THE *Improbable Quest* TO
Save THE *Corals* OF *Puerto Rico*

ISLANDS UNDER FIRE

Kevin McCarey

Copyright © 2012 by Kevin McCarey

ISBN 9780982694084

Book cover, layout and design by Nate Myers, Wilhelm Design
Editing by Linda Ellis

Printed in the United States of America

10 9 8 7 6 5 4 3 2 1

For Mary Frances

Contents

Praise *for* Islands Under Fire

"*Islands Under Fire* is a terrific read that held me spellbound from the first page. This is an exuberant tropical adventure regaled with gusto, and with exquisite prose that brings the colorful Puerto Rican characters to vivacious, chromatic life. McCarey's keen-eyed observation and understanding reflect a deep affection for Puerto Rico and the people of Vieques and Culebra, whose Caribbean paradise suffered decades as a bombing range."

—Christopher Baker,
Lowell Thomas Travel Writer of the Year

"Kevin McCarey, an outstanding writer and renowned film-maker, has a deep compassion for the natural world. His new book *Islands Under Fire* takes the reader on a wild, entertaining, and unforgettable ride. So compelling is the story that the lessons embedded in it about the vital need to conserve our marine resources and protect coral ecosystems are absorbed effortlessly. I urge you to read it."

—Chris Palmer, author, *Shooting in the Wild*

"I think it's terrific – funny, poignant, a good read."

—Mitchell Burgess, writer-producer,
Northern Exposure, The Sopranos

"Kevin McCarey is an imaginative talent with a gift for the magical and mystical. His writing reveals a rich understanding of Puerto Rico and its people – reveling in their humanity and their eccentricities."

—Vivian Schiller, chief, NBC News Digital

"Many of the books about the parlous condition of non-human life on earth currently being published engender such a bleak aura of disaster that the reader tends to be turned off. *Islands Under Fire* is an exception. Although it extols the urgent necessity of finding a new way of dealing with non-human life, it does not belabor the reader or preach at him. It gets across the message so skillfully imbedded in a damn good story that I for one could not put it down."

—Farley Mowat, author, *Never Cry Wolf,*
A Whale for the Killing

"It's kind of miraculous. Deep and mysterious and really fun."

—Robin Green, writer-producer,
Northern Exposure, The Sopranos

"In every phase of this fast moving, inspiring story, McCarey gleans his life's most essential moments, both hurtful and hilarious, nourishing himself for his next improbable adventure. *Islands Under Fire* is a new kind of narrative: part *"Liar's Club"* and part *"Lonely Planet"* bundled into one terrific book."

—David Hamlin, executive producer,
National Geographic Television

Acknowledgments

I would like to thank friends and colleagues T.C. Boyle, Scott Boylston, Mitchell Burgess, Chip Duncan, Sam Gilston, Robin Green, David Hamlin, Gail Krueger, Dave McGahee, Dave Ryan and Bryan Thompson for their unflagging encouragement. I'd also like to acknowledge Roberto Fuertes and David Hamby for their invaluable notes, and Linda Ellis for her meticulous editing. The support of literary agent William Reiss has been much appreciated. And I'm especially appreciative of the commitment and dedication of Frank Gromling, whose Ocean Publishing is a model of vision and integrity.

In Puerto Rico: *muchísimas gracias a* Frank Torres whose passion for the marine environment has been truly inspiring to me. And, closer to home, I raise a glass to my son Brett and the brothers McCarey for sharing a lifetime of misadventures with the intrepid captain. Of course, I am eternally grateful to Fran, my own enchanting muse.

The world's coral reefs are more endangered than ever. From climate change and overfishing, yes, but even worse: the acidification of our oceans which threatens all life in the sea. "One generation abandons the enterprises of another like stranded vessels," wrote Henry David Thoreau. We hope the book will prove Thoreau wrong, and inspire action from a new generation of conservationists, among them: Josephine and Madeleine McCarey.

Author's note: This is a memoir, but also a sea story. Names have been changed, and the events, while true, have been re-ordered and dramatized to better serve the narrative.

You will be no prophetic ship
of war, armed to defy the hurricane,
conquering the port, and dominating
waves and men, dauntless and brave;
but you will be like a tranquil little boat
that nudged on by perfumed breezes
rests in the ebb tide of the white shore.

—José Gautier Benítez, Puerto Rican poet

Prologue

We are underway at last. Seagulls squawk overhead, mocking the riot of colors that is the *Maroho,* a twenty-six-foot trawler painted pink and orange. Fredo, the mate, is on the bow, flaking down the lines in long, lazy figure eights and singing along with a portable radio. Thus a trio in perfect harmony becomes a slightly discordant quartet. The song is a romantic bolero: *Sin tu amor . . . todo es sufrir,* "Without your love . . . everything is suffering."

And I'm at the helm, guiding the boat across San Juan Bay to the mouth of the harbor and the open seas beyond. The boat rises and dips as we cross the steep wake of the Cataño Ferry carrying passengers to the Old City of San Juan. An elderly man on the stern studies us, wondering perhaps where our fishing outriggers are.

I ask Fredo to go below and check on José, our mechanic. José, it seems, has had another rough night. Heartbroken over

the loss of *la gringa,* he has self-prescribed some "medication"—
to ease the suffering, he says. To ease the pain of love. Now José
is passed out in the cabin. This is not good. We need José.

The first launching of the R/V *Maroho,* a few long months
ago, did not go well, despite the festive atmosphere. For the staff
of the fledgling Area of Natural Resources—part of Puerto Rico's Department of Public Works—the maiden voyage of their
first research vessel called for a celebration, and as we eased the
Maroho down the ramp, it was to the accompaniment of loud
applause and louder *salsa* music. But she quickly flooded with
seawater. The boat plug was missing, and the *Maroho* nearly
foundered in the shipping channel. The rum-soaked crowd
cheered anyway.

The main casualty was the spanking new inboard/outboard
engine. Although it has since been flushed and rebuilt, its re-
liability is questionable. But the urgency of our mission pre-
cludes a proper break-in period. If anything goes wrong with
the engine, we're depending on José to repair it.

We have reached the mouth of the harbor, and the Old
City is off the starboard bow. The *Maroho* enters the shadow
cast by the high bluff the city is built upon. San Juan is surrounded by ancient walls some forty feet tall and eleven feet
thick. Here and there along the ramparts stand sentry boxes
that seem to have sprouted like stone mushrooms. A little chapel marks the spot where centuries ago a miracle occurred. A
young rider, racing his friends down a cobbled street, couldn't
rein in his horse. Both horse and rider went over the wall to
what should have been certain death on the boulders far below.
But the boy's father cried out to the holy spirits to spare his

son's life. Incredibly, the boy survived. The chapel was built by a grateful father.

Now, from the roof of the chapel, a flock of white doves takes flight and disappears into the slate gray mist that hangs just above the city. The doves swoop out of the mist, their feathers imbued with an iridescent rose by the morning light.

"*Mágico,*" says Fredo. Yes, pure magic.

Writing of other Spanish islands in a distant sea, Herman Melville once observed that "this apparent fleetingness and unreality of the locality of the isles was most probably one reason for the Spaniards calling them the Encantada, or Enchanted Group." These are places where unseen powers cast their spells, where nothing is inevitable, where the best laid plans go awry.

"*Capitán,*" says Fredo. "You look worried."

"I'm not worried."

"You have that look."

"What look?"

"Have a mango. I brought them from *la finca,* my grandmother's farm."

"Maybe later," I say.

"These are the ones you really like. Sweet, juicy. Like a woman's . . . "

"Maybe later, Fredo, when we're out to sea."

"*Capitán,* I know you. When we're out to sea, you'll say 'Maybe later, when we're past El Morro.' And when we're past El Morro, you'll say 'Maybe later, when we're past Condado.' And when we're past Condado, you'll say—"

"Fredo, give me the friggin' mango."

"*Bueno.* You will thank me, *Capitán.* You will thank me."

I bite into a sliver of fruit. It's delicious.

"Thank you."

He knows me too well, this Fredo.

Just off our starboard bow, an imposing bronze monument overlooks the harbor: the tall, gaunt figure of the Bishop of San Juan accompanied by three torch-bearing maidens. It's called *La Rogativa,* "the procession." In 1797, Puerto Rico was under siege by British forces. Sir Ralph Abercrombie was confident of an easy victory. After all, he had a fleet of sixty warships and ten thousand battle-hardened troops, while the Spaniards had a small militia of mostly untrained civilians. San Juan seemed destined to fall. But the bishop spread the word throughout the city: men, women, and children were to gather that night at the cathedral. He would lead them in a candlelight procession along the great walls of the city. They would pray to St. Ursula of the Eleven Thousand Virgins for divine intercession. With eleven thousand heavenly spirits on their side, they would out-number the enemy by at least a thousand.

That night, British lookouts reported a great deal of com-motion in the Old City. Church bells were ringing, and count-less little flames were flickering in the streets. By midnight, the procession of flames had grown incredibly long. Abercrombie was alarmed. Clearly, reinforcements had arrived from some-where and in overwhelming numbers. Abercrombie blinked. The spell was cast. Legend has it that sometime after midnight he ordered his men to withdraw to their launches on the beach. By sunrise, all the troops had been ferried back to their ships. By noon, the British fleet had disappeared over the horizon;

they were headed back to England. The siege was over. The enchanted isle was spared.

Fredo is whacking the portable radio now. Everything's gone staticky.

"*Cabrón! Me cago en tu madre!*" Cuckold! I shit on your mother!

I have to smile. Fredo's occasional outbursts have taken my command of Spanish to levels I never dreamed of. The static disappears. Fredo strokes the radio. "I'm sorry," he says. "May the Virgin bless you."

As the *Maroho* heads toward the sun, we pass a long stretch of beach named Piñones for the wispy Australian pines that guard the dunes. Lacy branches sway in the breeze as if alerting the gods to our passing (the benevolent gods, one hopes). We are doing maybe six knots now, keeping the engine's revs low. I can hear one of the cylinders missing, and I consider rousing José. But soon the engine is running smoothly again. Perhaps there was a little water in the gas line, or a speck of dirt in the carburetor. Whatever it was, it's gone now, and the engine is purring like Eartha Kitt.

We cut through a wide band of brown, murky water, the effluent from the Rio Grande de Loíza. Two ebony-colored men are paying out a net from a small wooden boat; they pause to give us a gesture of blessing for a safe voyage.

Huts on stilts hug the eastern bank of the river. The village of Loíza Aldea was founded by freed slaves, and even today it's very African. This is where one comes to eat land crabs—minced, spiced, and folded into pastry shells. It is also where one comes to drink Palo Viejo rum—to divine excess, of course—and to don the horned coconut mask of the demon god and dance until the cock crows. It is where one buys vials of sacred amulets like the one Fredo bought to bring the *Maroho* luck. The vial contains a doll's eye, a sprig of parsley, the hair of a white goat, and paint flecks from a statue of the Virgin Mary. It dangles from the boat's radio antenna. The way things have been going, we need all the luck we can get.

Fredo breaks out pastry turnovers and a thermos of coffee.

"*Capitán?*"

"Yes, Fredo."

"*Pastelillos.*"

"I can see that."

"You should have one."

"I just had a mango."

"But these are made with papaya, which is very good for the eyes."

"My eyes are fine, Fredo."

"They're good for digestion too. You should have one before we eat lunch."

"It's seven o'clock in the morning. I'm not thinking about lunch right now."

"*Coño,*" he says. Damn! He's incredulous that I could be thinking of something other than lunch.

José is awake now but still bleary eyed, still crestfallen. Only a few days ago he was deliriously happy. At the time, *la gringa* was still enamored of him. An exchange student from New York, she was the most sexually adventurous woman he'd ever met. "She does it all," he said, overjoyed at finding her. "She does it all." But now she's dumped him, and he shakes his head despondently. "She did it all," he says. "She did it all."

The sun peeks up over the Luquillo Mountain Range. Its signature peak, El Yunque, is surrounded by rain forest and perpetually ringed with clouds. The Taíno Indians had great faith in the mountain. The gods who lived there shielded the island from the wrath of the storm god, *Huracán*. This time of year, hurricanes are rare, but it can still get very rough at sea. The trade winds shift to the northeast and stiffen, whipping up whitecaps. The seas also undulate with heavy swells generated by winter storms far to the north. From Puerto Rico to Nova Scotia there is nothing but a vast stretch of water, and any oceanic disturbance spreads like ripples in a pond. It is the fate of small islands to be forever at the mercy of immutable forces thousands of miles away.

Since Spanish colonial times, Puerto Rico has been a political vassal, subject to the whims of lords who ruled from afar. The nobles of Spain passed laws controlling trade, immigration, agriculture, education, and even social mores. It was decreed that when the islanders danced, only their fingers could touch. Yet somehow they found ways to subvert the rules through smuggling, piracy, and licentiousness. More than fingers touched.

Today, in 1970, it is the US government that controls Puerto Rico's affairs. While there are no longer laws against intimate dancing, there are other decrees that are just as absurd, and more odious. Among them, Executive Order 8684. Signed by President Franklin D. Roosevelt in 1941, the emergency order authorized the use of Culebra, a small island off Puerto Rico, for gunnery exercises by the military. The Navy purchased about a third of Culebra, as well as most of Vieques, another small island off Puerto Rico. Farms and homes were expropriated, and residents were forcibly relocated. Though World War II ended two decades ago, the orders to use both of these islands for target practice has never been rescinded, much to the chagrin of those who still live on them.

Culebra and Vieques are among some fifty islands, islets, and cays collectively known as the Spanish Virgin Islands. They are municipalities of Puerto Rico, yes, but in many ways they are worlds apart. While the mainland is densely populated, highly industrialized, and rife with slums and suburbs and traffic-choked highways, the Spanish Virgins are quiet, almost desolate places. Travel is by ferry or small boat. The people are subsistence farmers and fishers. Poor, yes, but spared the utter squalor of urban barrios. If the exploitable resources are few—and they are very few—there is one undeniable treasure: the marine environment. The lush mangrove nurseries and spectacular coral reefs comprise one of the richest ecosystems in the Caribbean.

Now, with the war raging in Vietnam, the Navy has decided to expand the target area and employ heavier fire power on Culebra. Precious mangroves and coral reefs, centuries in the making, will be blasted apart by missiles with names like Bulldog and Walleye and Shrike. And the island's remaining residents will be evicted.

But on Culebra, a mouse has roared. The island's feisty mayor has stood up to the military, setting into motion an improbable chain of events that will challenge the mightiest Navy in the world . And just as improbably, the R/V *Maroho* and her intrepid crew have been dispatched to play a key role in the unfolding drama.

As the *Maroho* rides the long, low swells of the open seas, I can see on the horizon a small freighter heading inbound from New York. It is the SS *Puerto Rico,* the ship that first brought me here. I was a twenty-two-year-old deck officer, burned out after too many voyages on decrepit merchant ships carrying missiles and munitions to Vietnam. Sustenance for the dragons of death. Now, two years later, I'm taking a little research boat to a small island imperiled by the same implacable gods of war I thought I'd eluded.

At six knots we should be off Cabo San Juan in about four hours. Culebra lies another seventeen nautical miles beyond the Cape. With any luck, we'll make it there before the trade winds kick up and the afternoon thunderstorms roll in. With any luck—and a little help from St. Ursula and the Eleven Thousand Virgins.

CHAPTER 1
El Capitán

God save me from still waters. The rough ones I can handle myself.
> —Puerto Rican proverb

The Water Quality Unit of the Environmental Engineering Division of the Area of Natural Resources of the Department of Public Works of the Executive Branch of the Commonwealth of Puerto Rico sits just off Avenida Ponce de Leon, on a sprawling campus of Spanish colonial buildings in various states of disrepair. I'm here to interview for the position of captain of their research vessel. It could be a steady job—and perhaps even meaningful.

It's been two years since I quit the SS *Puerto Rico* in San Juan. In the interim, I married a *puertorriqueña* named Sonia, and together we've produced baby Brett, now six months old. We live in Los Maestros, a suburb just outside the Old City.

The house is modest, powder blue, and solid cement. We drive a cranky Hudson, an English car I'd never even heard of before, that represents the sum total of our net worth. Sonia works for the Head Start Program, teaching preschoolers in Barrio Martín Peña, a slum that borders a fetid canal. And I've been working mostly as a port relief officer on freighters. In American ports, deck officers are hired to stand watch for their shipboard counterparts. It gives those who've been to sea some shore leave and, if it's their home port, some time to spend with their families. The relief jobs last as long as the ship is in port, anywhere from a few days to a few weeks. The work is dull as a night watchman's. God save me from still waters.

I meet with Mercedes Contreras, a woman in her thirties with a graduate degree in sanitation science. She has huge lips glistening with mica-flecked lipstick, and thick red hair swept up into a termite mound. Mercedes is the head of the Water Quality Unit, and she and her secretary, Llorlli (pronounced "Georgie"), comprise its only staff.

"Everything is so new here," she says in flawless English. "Except the buildings."

She's fanning herself with my resume, the electricity having crapped out just moments before my interview began. Not that it matters; there's no air-conditioning anyway, and the ceiling fans are missing a few blades. Mercedes seems very bright, if a bit academic; she speaks a blend of bureaucratese and scientificese. Her sentences are peppered with phrases like "forcing function" and "coliform count" and "optimal implementation" and "particulate matter." I don't understand half of what she's talking about, but the gist seems to be that as a US commonwealth, Puerto Rico is subject to the same legal standards as the mother country, as well as to the growing political pressure to clean up the environment. The Water Quality Unit has recently been created to study ocean pollution around the island. Hence, the need for a research vessel.

During my interview with Mercedes Contreras she expounds on "geopolitical realities" and "zeolite processes" and "sludge aeration factors" but says not a word about the captain's job.

I meet with architect Gabriel Ferrer of the Environmental Design Unit, a tall, pensive man with a rich baritone voice and a keen interest in the teachings of the Indian philosopher Krishnamurti. Gabriel and I philosophize for an hour over coffee, and it is a stimulating conversation, but the subject of the captain's position never comes up.

Next I interview with geologist Ambrosio Freyre of the Mineral Resources Unit. This too is a pleasant chat. He recalls his geological peregrinations around the island, and he tells many a good dirty joke, including one about a woman and a doorknob. But Freyre suffers from bilharzia, a disease caused by a parasite, prevalent in the rivers, that infects the kidneys and liver and causes drowsiness and ultimately death. He nods off just as I bring up the subject of the captain's job.

"Do you know," asks my next interviewer, Rafael Cruz-Cruz, "that there are manatees in Puerto Rico?"

"No sir," I reply. "I didn't know that."

"Well, there are. Many of them. In Fajardo. In Ceiba. In Jobos Bay. They love our bays and rivers. Scientists come from all over the world to study our manatees. They are magnificent animals. *Magnífico!*" He pounds his desk. Cruz-Cruz, a former artillery officer, is brimming with enthusiasm. He is a chemical engineer and the driving force behind both the water-quality study and the construction of the research vessel on which I will serve as captain. That is, if I'm hired. None of my interviewers, gracious as they've been, have given any indication that I will be.

"Do you know," says Cruz-Cruz, "that Puerto Rico has more of its original flora and fauna than Cuba? Than Jamaica? Than the Dominican Republic? Than Haiti—poor souls?"

"No sir, I did not know that."

"It is true! We have preserved more of our environment than all the big islands of the Caribbean. But we still have much work to do. The struggle continues!" He pounds his desk again. I like this man. I like his passion. But to get down to business . . .

"I was wondering about the research vessel," I say. "The one that I would be captain of. Should I be hired, that is."

"Aha! *Bueno!* I'm glad you asked me that. Now let me see . . ." He flips through my resume. "You are from New York?"

"Yes, sir. Small town in the Hudson Valley. Across the river from West Point." *Appalachia on the Hudson. Not far from where they threw stones at opera singer Paul Robeson.*

"I see. You didn't want to go to West Point?"

"No, sir. I wanted to go to sea. I used to watch the freighters heading downriver, and I'd wonder where they were going. I figured, wherever it was, it would be an adventure." *Or misadventure.*

"So you went to a merchant marine academy."

"New York Maritime. It's where I got my third mate's license."

"What did you do as a third mate?"

"At sea, I stood watch on deck. In port, I supervised the loading and unloading of cargo." *Chase bar girls, smoke dope, howl at the moon.*

"On the big ships."

"Not so big. C-class freighters and Victory cargo ships. They were built during World War II."

"And where did you sail to?"

"Vietnam mostly. We were required to sail three years in the 'merch' to satisfy our active-duty requirements for the Navy. Most of us ended up on ships carrying missiles and munitions to Saigon, Cam Ranh Bay, DaNang."

"This was dangerous."

"At times, yes." *As when a missile broke loose in a cargo hold. Or when crated ammo began firing spontaneously. Or when containers of Agent Orange sprang leaks. Of course, the dangers we faced were nothing compared to those faced by the weapons' intended targets: Vietnamese peasants. So let's not go there.*

"You navigated by the stars?"

"Yes sir. And by the sun."

"Very good." He goes to his work table, where blueprints, sketches, and charts are scattered everywhere. He pulls a big crate from underneath the table. "I have something to show you. It just came in today." He reaches into the crate and carefully lifts out a huge magnetic compass.

"What do you think?" he asks. The compass has a liquid-filled brass bowl with a nine-inch compass card, and it's the size of one you'd find on the bridge of a five-hundred-foot freighter.

"It's, uh, substantial looking."

"It is the biggest. It is the best. I did much research into this compass. In oceanography, navigational accuracy is very, very important. The bigger the compass, the more accurate it is."

"That makes sense, all other factors considered."

"Aha! So you agree. Good. *Bueno!* Do you know how to box the compass?" He's referring to the naming of all thirty-two points of the compass in clockwise order, a navigation ritual from the days of sail.

"Yes, I do."

"Will you box the compass for me?"

"Sure. North. North by east. North north east. North east. North east by east—"

Cruz-Cruz's eyes are closed, as if he is listening to a favorite poem or aria.

"—east north east. East by north. East . . ." and so on.

"*Magnífico!* Very nice. Would you like to hold it?"

"Sir?"

"The compass. Would you like to hold it in your hands?"

"OK." He hands me the compass.

"Careful," he warns. It's damned heavy—about thirty pounds.

"If you drop it, you're fired," Cruz-Cruz says with a smile.

And that's how I know I've been hired.

We celebrate my new job with Sonia's family. Her mother Doña Rita has cooked up a feast of steak and onions, rice and beans, grilled plantains, and avocados picked from their backyard tree. The steak is for everyone but me; for me, it's fried chicken. Not that I wouldn't enjoy the flank steak that's been marinated in garlic, oil, vinegar, and adobe spices, then lightly grilled and smothered in sautéed onions; it's just that I once mentioned to Doña Rita how much I loved her fried chicken and since then, whenever we eat at her home, which is frequently, I'm served fried chicken. It can get frustrating, munching on a chicken wing and watching the others feast on roast pig, stewed goat, or flank steak. But there is no polite way to decline the chicken. Doña Rita has made it especially for me. Sonia's older brother, Adaír, knows my dilemma and gets a big kick out of it.

"You're gonna walk like a chicken. Squawk like a chicken. You're gonna grow feathers, man," he laughs. "You got the ass, man. You really got the ass." That's his favorite expression. It's something he picked up while serving in the Army in Vietnam, along with "Don't panic!" and "Yo, mutha fugga!" He also came back with an outsized Afro that's the scandal of the family.

Sonia's sister, Ivette, is a shy, bookish teenager who reminds me of Laura in *The Glass Menagerie;* she dreams of being a pharmacist and working for the neighborhood drugstore. Brother Edgardo, "Egui," at sixteen is the youngest, and he's a strikingly handsome kid. He lives in a nocturnal world of his own, riding his bicycle all night long—no one knows where—and sleeping all day.

Doña Rita worries about all her family, but now that her son-in-law has found steady work—and with the government no less, *qué bueno!*—there's reason to celebrate.

"I was praying to the Virgin every day," she tells me. Doña Rita is a frail-looking woman with huge liquid eyes that belie an iron will. She teaches Spanish literature in a high school, and on shelves throughout her house there are Don Quixote statuettes, gifts from her students.

"I was praying she would give you this work. And see? The Virgin listened."

Her husband, Emilio, prays to Bacchus. An unemployed diamond cutter, he's been out celebrating on his own somewhere and doesn't show up until after we've all eaten. "Brrrrett!" he says, bathing his new grandson with the fumes of exhaled rum as he kisses the baby on the forehead. Then he takes his rightful place at the head of the table, bellows for service, and passes out as Doña Rita ladles the first spoonful of rice onto his plate.

"So . . . You are *El Capitán!*" Adaír says to me with playful derision. "How big is your boat, *Capitán?*"

"I have no idea."

"You should know these things," he says. "You are . . . *El Capitán!*"

"I am happy you have the work," says Doña Rita. "But I wish it was not on some boat. The ocean makes me very nervous. You have to watch out for the big fishes that can eat you. And the big waves that can drown you."

Puerto Ricans have always had ambivalent feelings towards the sea. Few of my Puerto Rican friends even know how to swim. The beach is a place where people gather to picnic, to talk, to listen to music. Few wear swimsuits; many are content to wade in the shallows fully clothed. The Spanish colonial powers discouraged local seamanship, portraying the ocean as a world of sharks and cutthroats—the better to keep the restless populace from sailing off to more prosperous colonies.

The first Spanish colonists longed to abandon the island and go elsewhere—to the Viceroyalties of New Granada (Colombia), New Spain (Mexico), and Peru, where gold and silver abounded. "God take me to Peru!" was the cry. But emigration was forbidden. Spain needed to keep a presence on the island to prevent other Europeans from laying claim to it. The governor instituted a strict penalty for people caught trying to leave: they would have their feet cut off.

Once, when a Spanish warship arrived, the governor begged the ship's captain to leave some men behind to bolster the meager garrison. The soldiers were ordered to draw lots, and forty men were compelled to stay. "They wept at the thought of remaining there," wrote the captain.

The island's settlers were not fishers or sailors but rather cattlemen from Castile or farmers from Andalucia or slaves from Africa. They planted sugar and ginger, raised pigs and cattle, cut native hardwoods, and foraged for medicinal herbs. The rich ocean bounty of fish and shellfish and crustacea was mostly ignored. In time, Puerto Rico became more isolated from the sea as fewer and fewer ships came into port. In the last twenty-five years of the sixteenth century, only eight Spanish ships visited San Juan.

But the island had other, less desirable, visitors from the sea. French corsairs like François le Clerc, the original "Peg Leg," raided the seaside settlements on the south coast, sacking and burning them. The Dutch also raided, stealing salt from the pans of Salinas—the better to preserve their herring. With every attack, coastal towns moved further and further inland.

To protect San Juan, work was begun on a fortress on a high bluff overlooking the bay: Castillo de San Felipe del Morro. "The forte, when it is ended," wrote Governor Diego Mendez de Valdez in 1590, "will be the strongest that his Majestie hath in all the Indies." Constructed with stones brought as ballast in Spanish galleons, it took more than half a century to build. When complete, it was grander than any medieval castle in Spain, towering 160 feet above the sea.

But the imposing presence of El Morro did not deter the English, who in 1598 besieged the fortress for six months until the Spaniards ran out of firepower and men. The English pillaged San Juan and ran off with a thousand cases of sugar, a hundred tons of ginger, and every church bell in the city.

In response, Spanish authorities ordered the construction of a great wall around San Juan. A hundred and fifty years later it was complete. But no wall could keep out the tropical storms that rolled in from the sea. Since the European settlement there have been more than eighty-five hurricanes in Puerto Rico. They have had a profound effect on island history, decimating coffee haciendas in the nineteenth century and sugar plantations in the twentieth, and thereby ending for all time the important role of these two crops in the island's economy.

One of the most violent hurricanes, San Narciso, swept in from the east in 1867. It was small, intense, and fast moving, killing a thousand islanders in a single day. Then, only ten days after San Narciso, a mysterious force sucked all the water out of Yabucoa Bay. Within minutes, a massive tidal wave some twenty feet high roared back into the bay, sending a deadly wall of water over the town and leaving in its wake an arena of death and destruction.

And so, throughout Puerto Rico's history, the sea has continually brought bad things to the island: pirates and invaders, hurricanes and tidal waves—or as Doña Rita would say, the big fishes that can eat you, and the big waves that can drown you.

CHAPTER 2
Paradise Lost

All these islands are very beautiful, lush with salubrious waters and full of great trees stretching up to the stars.
   —Christopher Columbus, letter to Queen Isabella

The United States has just held its first Earth Day. In San Francisco, Mayor Joseph Alioto proclaimed

As inhabitants of this Earth, Earthians, we need a day to celebrate our global unity and destiny. . . . a special day to remember Earth's tender seedlings of life and people; a day for planting trees and flowers; a day for cleaning streams and wooded glens. . . .

Earth Day was celebrated on April 22, 1970, all over the country. Actor celebrities Paul Newman and Ali MacGraw took the podium to condemn the despoiling of the environ-

ment, while folksinger Pete Seeger roused Earthians with ren-
ditions of "This Land is Your Land" and "Festival of Flowers"
and "Garbage":

> Garbage . . . garbage!
> We're filling up the sea with garbage . . . garbage!

All in all, some twenty million people participated in Earth
Day. It was an astonishing success. President Richard Nixon
was jarred into taking action, and within days the idea for the
Environmental Protection Agency was born. Since then Congress has enacted a flurry of legislation to clean up the nation's
air and water. Now Puerto Rico, too, must deal with the issue.

"Puerto Ricans love garbage so much," Lenny Bruce said,
"they'll steal it from next door and put it in front of their house."
A mean jibe, yes, but one that's hard to dispute if you've spent
any time on the island. There's crap everywhere: roadsides are
littered with bottles and cans and Clorox containers; streams are
clogged with used tires and old refrigerators and plastic bags.
Even the San Cristóbal Canyon, a spectacular natural wonder,
is so full of junked cars you can barely see the river below.

But there's a growing awareness here as well. And on Earth
Day Puerto Ricans rallied to clean up their island. School kids
sang "La Borinqueña," the lilting anthem of Puerto Rico. The
English translation goes something like this:

> The land of Borinquen
> where I was born
> is a flowery garden

of magical brilliance.
A sky always clear
serves as a canopy
and peaceful lullabies are sung
by the waves at her feet.
When on her shores Columbus arrived,
he exclaimed with admiration,
"Oh! Oh! Oh! This is the
beautiful land I'm searching for.
It is Borinquen, the daughter
of the sea and the sun."

"La Borinqueña" is a lovely song that takes its melody from a nineteenth-century serenade sung in festivals across the island and its rhythm from the *habanera,* a type of Cuban dance music. The poet Manuel Fernández Juncos (after whom a busy boulevard in Santurce is named) wove the lyrics of his poem "La Tierra de Borinquen" into the *habanera.* It can be performed as a slow, stately dance or as a stirring march. Borinquen refers to the original Taíno Indian name for the island, and it evokes the tropical Eden that Columbus first set eyes upon.

Columbus wrote that the earth is shaped like a woman's breast, and that on its nipple were the islands of the Indies. He described the Caribbean as a place of perpetual summer, where birds sing all winter long and trees never lose their leaves. A bountiful place with waters teeming with fish and lush forests filled with easy pickings. But it was the demeanor of the "gentle" and "friendly" naked Indians that convinced him he was at the very gates of heaven.

The Taíno Indians lived in Cuba, in Hispaniola, and on the island they called Borinquen, "land of the great chief," which Columbus named San Juan but which soon became known as Puerto Rico. Unlike the combative Caribs of the Lesser Antilles, the Taínos were peace loving. *Taíno* means "the good people" in their language. Their villages were built along the coast, where they fished and farmed. They grew tapioca, sweet potatoes, and cassava, staples in island cuisine even today. They lived in thatched-roof cottages of a type that housed many Puerto Ricans right up until the twentieth century. They played a kind of soccer in ceremonial fields called *bateyes* (unlike the Aztecs and Mayans, the Taínos did not decapitate or cannibalize the losers). They loved to get high on a hallucinogenic powder called cohoba, which when consumed can invert the world so that people, animals and objects appear upside down, and movements and gestures are reversed. They also loved to play music with the maracas, güiros, and kettle drums that drive Latin rhythms today. The Taínos were the original flower children.

For a thousand years, the Taínos thrived in Borinquen. But thirty years after Columbus's arrival, they had been all but wiped out by European guns, germs, and steel. The few who survived fled to the mountains; their gene pool runs strong in many country folk today.

Now millions of people crowd Puerto Rico, making the island the second most densely populated place on earth. The "flowery garden" where "a sky always clear serves as a canopy" is choking on the fumes from hundreds of thousands of cars and trucks. The beaches where "peaceful lullabies are sung by the waves" are awash with diapers and condoms and sanitary napkins.

Still, there has been a sea change in attitude toward the environment. A company plans to mine for copper in the mountains of Adjuntas, threatening to pollute the purest streams on the island with tailings and toxic waste; Puerto Rican conservationists are taking legal action to stop the mining. Squatters build vacation huts in the bioluminescent bay at La Parguera, dumping raw sewage into one of the world's most fragile ecosystems; Puerto Ricans are calling for government intervention to stop the building. The Bonus Nuclear Power Plant has allowed radioactive contamination to seep into the substrate of the northwest coast; Puerto Ricans are rallying to close the plant. The protesters' gatherings are very Caribbean in flavor, with food, music, and dancing, but their goals are clear, their commitment is real, and their energy is infectious.

"The problem we have is what to do with all the *caca*," says Cruz-Cruz on my first day of work.

"The *caca*."

"*Sí*, the *caca*. The poop." He goes to a US Geological Survey topographical map of Puerto Rico that's pinned on the wall.

"You know what they say: *Caca* flows downhill. It is true. Look." He taps the map forcibly for dramatic effect.

Cruz-Cruz still has the bearing and the buzz cut of a military man. He taps towns and villages on the map as if they are enemy positions. "All the *caca* from all these places flows into the streams, and the streams flow into the rivers, and the rivers flow into the sea."

He taps the cities of San Juan, Ponce, Mayagüez, Humacao. "And on the coast, all the *caca* from the cities flows into
the sea. We have two and a half million people on this island.
That is two and a half million *cacas* every day. Two and a half
million *cacas* flowing into the sea and onto our beaches. That
is not acceptable. We love our beaches. The tourists love our
beaches. Do you like our beaches?"

I *did*, I'm thinking. "Yes, I love the beaches," I say.

"Very good. Me too. So. *Bueno.* How do we save our beaches?" He taps along the pencil lines he's drawn on the map, lines
that extend out from the coastline like spokes of a wheel. "With
big . . . long . . . pipes . . . like these. Sewage outfalls. Here and
here and here and here and here and so on. Sixteen of them. All
around the island. Each one will extend miles out to sea. There,
all the *caca* will be discharged and carried away by the ocean
currents. With any luck it will all wash up on Cuba's beaches.
Hahaha!"

There's a great rivalry between Puerto Ricans and Cubans,
and the very thought of Puerto Rican feces washing up on Cuban beaches is irresistible to Cruz-Cruz.

"I'm just kidding, of course," he says. "The Dominican Republic is in the way."

But the real problem is that no one knows exactly where
the discharged sewage will end up. The prevailing currents have
not been charted since the turn of the nineteenth century.

The last survey of the island waters was conducted in 1899
by the US Fish Commission aboard the SS *Fish Hawk.* She was
a two-masted schooner outfitted as an ocean-going marine fish
hatchery. Otter and beam trawls netted fish specimens, while

dredges dragged the sea bottom for benthic marine organisms. The biologists collected snappers and groupers, lobsters and crabs, clams and mussels, soft corals and hard corals, round worms and flat worms. On their return to the States, they published reports with titles like "The Brachyura and Macrura of Porto Rico" and "Description of Two New Leeches From Porto Rico," complete with richly detailed illustrations. The reports were forgotten not long after they were filed away in the vast dungeons of the Smithsonian Institution.

Now the Area of Natural Resources will undertake the first oceanographic survey in more than seventy years. A team of marine scientists is being recruited. A research vessel is being built and outfitted. And a captain has been hired, a twenty-four-year-old gringo who's been given the job because Cruz-Cruz likes that he is a "blue water sailor" who has crossed the oceans dozens of times.

"I imagine you have seen everything: whales and sharks and orcas and such," he said to me during my interview.

In fact, one rarely sees much marine life far out at sea. One sees mostly birds, and these only occasionally. I used to bring along a big book of seabirds filled with colorful paintings and drawings. It was a rare treat to identify a shearwater gliding overhead, or a white-tailed tropicbird poised in midair and shivering from end to end, or storm petrels paddling just above the sea surface as if trying to walk on water. I remember when I saw my first albatross while sailing on the SS *Beaver Victory* south of the Hawaiian Islands. The largest flying creature on earth, with its thirteen-foot wingspan, the albatross is the legendary bird of The Rime of the Ancient Mariner:

At length did cross an Albatross,
Thorough the fog it came;
As if it had been a Christian soul,
We hailed it in God's name.

"Jesus H. Christ," said the crew of the SS *Beaver Victory*, hailing it in God's name. "Look at fucking size of that thing."

Sighting marine mammals is also not as common as you'd think. It's always a thrill when they appear. I remember seeing sperm whales, off the Azores, swimming upside down, their narrow jaws chomping at the air; and humpback whales poised vertically, their tail flukes jutting high out of the water. Once, in the Pacific, I saw a dazzling performance by a large pod of spinner dolphins that leaped completely out of the water and spun like ice skaters performing a triple axel. These were all rare sightings.

There are fewer fishes out in blue waters as well. Yes, there are tunas and billfish and dorados, but nowhere near the number of species that inhabit the shallows. The richest ecosystems are nearer to shore, in the estuaries and coral reefs, on the continental shelves, and along coasts that feature upwelling. Here the abundance of nutrients provides sustenance for the tiny creatures that create the great oceanic food chain.

When sailing in these inshore waters, I would toss a bucket from the ship and haul up seawater and strain it through fine cheesecloth. Then I'd view the plankton through a cheap microscope I'd picked up in Yokosuka. I made sketches of their myriad shapes. The phytoplankton (tiny plants) look like aliens from another planet, and the zooplankton (tiny animals) like the aliens' spaceships. I filled a notebook with rough drawings of plankton and jellies and seabirds and marine mammals, but it was simply the work of an amateur enthusiast.

Now, that amateur will be working with real marine scientists on a survey that could actually prove useful.

"I don't like work—no man does," wrote Joseph Conrad in *Heart of Darkness,* "but I like what is in the work—the chance to find yourself."

CHAPTER 3
Navigational Hazards

A momentous but until then overlooked fact was making itself apparent: I had inadvertently brought myself with me to the island.

—Alain de Botton, *The Art of Travel*

Puerto Rico Yachts is a big, sprawling place with huge work sheds and open yards filled with boats in various stages of construction. Workers in surgical masks labor in clouds of sawdust and fiberglass to the drone and buzz and whine of sanders and saws and drills. This is where our research vessel is being constructed.

Cruz-Cruz and I meet with the foreman, a heavyset man named Bruno, in his office. He says the timing of our arrival is perfect. Today the hull will be lifted from its fiberglass mold. I don't know much about ship construction, but I'm surprised to hear that our research vessel is made of fiberglass. Most are steel hulled.

Bruno spreads out a blueprint. I glance over his shoulder, but it's hard to make sense of the blueprint with its abstract geometric shapes, its labels in Spanish, its scribbled dimensions. I try to visualize the vessel; I wonder how big she is. I remember seeing the R/V *Atlantis* off the Azores. She's the ketch-rigged schooner of the Woods Hole Oceanographic Institution and she's about 140 feet long. Jacques Cousteau's R/V *Calypso*, a former mine sweeper, is also about 140 feet. Some of the smaller research vessels include WHOI's yawl-rigged *Caryn*, a former smuggler, at 98 feet, Oregon State University's *Acona* at 80 feet, and the University of Miami's *Calanus* at 68 feet. Curiously, the LOA—the length overall—on the blueprint of our vessel is blank.

Cruz-Cruz points out a square that's full of circles and trapezoids.

"Aha! The main cabin. Very nice," he says. "I can see the scientists working up their data in there. Salinity, temperature, dissolved oxygen, pH, whatever."

He then runs his finger along a rectangle filled with triangles and rhombi.

"*Ah, sí.* The main deck. *Bueno.*" He indicates where the water sampling bottles will go, where the cable winch will be installed, where the bathythermograph boom will be rigged, and where the dive gear locker and the racks for scuba tanks will be built.

As Cruz-Cruz chatters on, the vessel in the blueprint comes to life, and I can see oceanographers and biologists and scuba divers scurrying about, lowering instruments, working up samples, and plunging into the depths.

Until the nineteenth century there was no "ocean science" to speak of. If anything, ships' captains kept their knowledge of prevailing winds and currents to themselves as a kind of trade secret. Even the heavily trafficked Gulf Stream was not charted until 1770. It took an insatiably curious postmaster named Ben Franklin to do so. He had already set down his observations on electricity, smallpox, whirlwinds, insects, evaporation, geology, and Scottish tunes. Now he wondered why eastbound vessels carrying mail across the Atlantic made quicker time than westbound vessels. Franklin made eight transatlantic crossings, and en route he took temperature samplings and noted the absence or prevalence of gulfweed in the waters. He combined his observations with those of his cousin Captain Timothy Folger to create his classic chart of the Stream.

Another American, Lt. Matthew Fontaine Maury, undertook the first organized study of the oceans in the 1830s. He worked in the US Navy's Depot of Charts and Instruments, and there began to sift through ships' logs for data on winds and currents. He encouraged ships' captains to take deep ocean soundings using an apparatus with a detachable weight. In 1854 he created the first bathymetric chart of the North Atlantic. A year later he published the first textbook on oceanography, *The Physical Geography of the Sea*.

In 1872 the British ship HMS *Challenger* set out on a major oceanographic expedition. The *Challenger* was a 226-foot steamship with a crew of 243 and a scientific party of six. For three and a half years, the scientists explored sixty-nine thousand square miles of the Atlantic, Pacific, and Southern oceans. Data were collected on salinities, temperatures, and depths; on winds and currents; on bottom contours; and on marine life. It took fifteen years and fifty large volumes to publish all the information, and it is still an invaluable reference work for today's ocean studies. There will probably never again be a single-ship expedition of the size and scope of the HMS *Challenger.*

The sea has not always been kind to research vessels. In 1839 the *Sea Gull* disappeared in the Southern Ocean with 28 men aboard. In 1881 the *Jeannette* was trapped, then crushed, by Arctic ice; 19 men froze to death in the lifeboats. More recently the *Gulf Stream,* a fifty-five-foot research vessel, sank off the coast of Maine with six scientists aboard.

Now there are hundreds of research vessels actively engaged in marine research. The Russians have the most by far, followed by the US, Japan, and the UK. For all this effort, we still know less about the ocean than we do about the moon. The sea is our last frontier.

Our own study will focus on only a few hundred miles of coastline and is not likely to make history. Still, I'm pretty enthused as Bruno leads us toward a huge shed at Puerto Rico Yachts. Ours is the biggest boat they've ever made, he says, and it's been a learning process. That's not what you want to hear, but the candor is appreciated.

And there she is. With a crane, the hull is lifted from its mold like a turkey being lifted from a roasting pan.

"*Magnífico!*" says Cruz-Cruz as it hovers in the air.

All twenty-six feet of it.

My first thought is, Jesus, how are we going to fit all those scientists, all that instrumentation, all that gear on that little boat? Then I remember the balsa canoes of the Polynesians. They were only about forty feet long, yet they transported dozens of settlers with their pigs and breadfruit and taro throughout the wide Pacific. And the Polynesians were very large people. Still, twenty-six feet seems awfully small for a research vessel.

The hull is set on a cradle between the cabin and the bridge, which are sitting on sawhorses. At some point the three parts of the boat will be fitted together like plastic LEGO bricks and fused in place.

"So," says Cruz-Cruz, "what do you think of the colors?"

The colors. The colors of the boat are not what I would I have chosen. The upper hull is the shocking pink of the vinyl miniskirts worn by the bar girls of Calle Luna. Below the waterline it's a vibrant orange flecked with mica, like Mercedes's lipstick.

"I picked the colors myself," says Cruz-Cruz.

"They're . . . vivid," I say.

"*Exacto!* They are very vivid. The better to see the boat from a distance. Let's say your engine has died. The boat is drifting. The radio has failed because you have no power. And now comes a big storm." He's no longer Cruz-Cruz, chemical engineer. He's 1st Lt. Cruz-Cruz, coming to the rescue. "But you are in luck. We notice you are overdue at the dock and we send up a plane to search for you. Did you know I have a pilot's license?"

"No, I didn't know that."

"Well, I do. I am a licensed pilot for single-engine planes. And I know how difficult it is to see things from the air, especially on the surface of the sea. Do you know how hard it is to spot a boat when the sea is rough?"

"I imagine it's not easy."

"It is very difficult. But the colors on *that* boat can be seen for miles. That's a fact. I researched it. The Coast Guard has done studies. Pink. Orange. Those colors can be seen for miles. Those colors will save your life, *Capitán*. They will save your life!"

He has a point, I suppose.

Bruno tells us there's still much work to do: wiring for shore and engine power, plumbing for the galley and marine head, carpentry for the main cabin and stateroom, electronics for the bridge, and installation of the boat's engine. The engine, a Chrysler inboard/outboard, has not yet arrived from the mainland. When I ask how long this will all take, the foreman smiles and says, "Don't worry, man. We will finish your boat."

"Our *capitán* is ready to go now," laughs Cruz-Cruz. "He needs to make a drug run to Colombia. Hahaha!"

Later, Cruz-Cruz and I stop in a café for some beers. I voice my concerns about the size of the boat. It's not only a practical issue—will we have room enough to work?—but a safety issue as well.

"For what we need to do," says Cruz-Cruz, "measuring the currents, the chemistry, the coliforms, the boat will be more than sufficient. You will see."

What I don't share with him is my true concern. All my seagoing experience has been on large ships. I'm not sure I can translate that experience into running such a small boat in un-familiar waters. As Jack London put it:

> The small-boat sailor is the real sailor. . . . He must know
> about tides and rips and eddies, bar and channel markings,
> and day and night signals; he must be wise in weather-lore;
> and he must be sympathetically familiar with the peculiar
> qualities of his boat which differentiate it from every other
> boat that was ever built and rigged. . . . A man can sail in
> the forecastles of big ships all his life and never know what
> real sailing is.

Cruz-Cruz sets the compass on the table. He gazes into it as if it is a crystal ball and he is divining the boat's future.

"The compass is the soul of the ship," wrote Victor Hugo in *Toilers of the Sea*. The novel is about a fisherman who must salvage a small vessel that has run aground on a reef.

I've been given a space in an empty building in the Area of Natural Resources. The weathered stucco edifice was built in the late nineteenth century and is under renovation. Workmen are busying about, carrying plywood and drywall sheets, pinewood planks and two-by-four studs. There's a cacophony of sawing and hammering and "*Ay, coños!*" when someone whacks a finger. Every now and then a workman will ask me to steady one end of a drywall sheet while he hammers it in place. At coffee time they offer me *brazos gitanos*, "gypsy arms," a kind of cream roll cake. My office has only one finished wall, the outside one. The other three walls are simply frames. Three-by-five cards indicate where things will eventually go: *abanico* (wall fan), *puerta* (door), *luz* (light). I feel as if I'm inside a blueprint.

Tacked up on a sheet of drywall is US Coast and Geodetic Survey Chart 920. The chart shows Puerto Rico and its surrounding islands. I've drawn sixteen lines jutting out from the coast, representing transects lines for the oceanographic study. These lines are where the sewage outfalls will eventually go. There are four transects on each coast, and I need to get familiar with the waters surrounding each of them.

A shallow shelf extends a few miles out from the south and east coasts but hugs closely to shore on the north coast. There, the bottom drops off precipitously to the Puerto Rico Trench more than five miles deep, the deepest part of the Atlantic Ocean. To go down with your ship out there is to descend into a lightless nether world inhabited by a phantasmagoria of bizarre creatures from vampire squid to triplewart seadevils. Not the place you want to spend eternity.

I sit in a foldout chair at a foldout table perusing nautical reference books and periodicals covered with layers of drywall dust. There are copies of the *Tide Tables* as well as the *Tidal Current Tables*. The *Tide Tables* measure the periodic rise and fall of the water level, while the *Tidal Current Tables* give the speed and direction of the tide's flow. The tides are modest, mostly about a foot in vertical range. But the tidal currents can be formidable, up to three and a half knots, as strong as the Gulf Stream.

For more detailed descriptions of the harbors, reefs, currents, and navigational aids, there is the *Coast Pilot for Puerto Rico and the Virgin Islands*. It is the most useful reference, though it can be somewhat alarmist in tone. It warns of strong winds blowing over a long fetch of water. Of extreme waves reaching forty feet or more. Of tropical storms bringing torrential rains, reducing visibility to zero.

Each coast has its own particular navigational hazards. On the west coast is the treacherous Mona Passage, where the weather is turbulent and a strong three-and-a-half knot current has been reported. The north coast is just as uninviting, with northeast winds that pile up heavy seas and breakers.

The east coast, the *Coast Pilot* warns, is very irregular; its rocky bluffs and numerous small bays should be navigated only with local knowledge. The south coast has fringing reefs close to shore that make landing in most places difficult and often dangerous; these waters, too, should be sailed only with local knowledge. All our survey lines lie within these treacherous waters.

The words "local knowledge" are like a mantra in the *Coast Pilot*. It occurs to me that it would really be helpful to hire a mate for the boat who knows these waters. A fisherman, a "yachtie," or even a surfer. Cruz-Cruz says he knows just the man.

"His father is the head of the Sewage Authority," he enthuses. "The nut does not fall far from the tree. Remember that."

I'm sure he means that as a good thing.

CHAPTER 4
Love and Anarchy

It might in the hands of the English or Dutch be rendered a paradise on Earth, but the Present Inhabitants are Mere Devils.
—Eighteenth-century English visitor to Puerto Rico

Alfredo Lopez-León shows up in ragged shorts, a tie-dyed shirt, and flip-flops that reveal the hairy feet of a Hobbit. He's a few years younger than me, maybe twenty years old, and he has the most engaging smile.

"*Buenos dias, Capitán.* I am Alfredo. My friends call me Freddy or Fredo." We make small talk. Like a Hobbit, too, Fredo loves food, drink, and music—and a good pipe, I suspect. It's hard not to like the man. Though I have some doubts about his credentials.

"Ever work on a boat, Fredo?"

"No. Never."

"Have you spent much time on the water? Like fishing, maybe?"

"Not really. I don't like to fish. You see them flopping about with the hook in their mouths. It makes me sad."

"I can appreciate that. But are you at all familiar with the local waters? You know, the inlets and bays, the rocks and reefs."

He ponders this a moment.

"I like the beaches; I like the waves."

"Great. Do you surf?"

"No."

"No. OK. No fishing, no surfing. Can you swim, Fredo?"

"Oh, yes. Front stroke. Side stroke. I can't do the back stroke, but I can hold my breath underwater for a long time."

"Good, great, terrific. If the boat sinks that will come in handy. How about mechanics? Ever work on any engines, Fredo?"

"No. Never."

"Right . . . Look. The job, as you know, is to work as a mate on a boat. That means maintaining the gear, making sure the fuel tanks are topped off, swabbing decks, helping out with the rigging—you know, boat stuff. And I could sure use help navigating the local waters. Can you tell me why I should hire you, Fredo?"

He breaks out that winning smile. "I can drive, man. I can really drive."

And he can. Puerto Rico may be one of the most perilous places to drive a car in the Western Hemisphere. It's like a demolition derby. But Fredo is fearless. He may look like a Hobbit, but behind the wheel, Fredo is a fiery-eyed Orc. We're in this big white wagon, an International Harvester Travelall owned by the Area of Natural Resources, and we're driving around the city in search of supplies for the boat. Fredo roars up one-way streets the wrong way. Barrels through red lights and stop signs. Zooms around buses, trucks, and wagons on blind alleys, all the while honking the horn and pounding the wheel to a *salsa* beat and swearing up a storm.

"*Coño! Pendejo! Cabrón! Carajo!*"

He slows only at the sight of a woman. Then he slows to a crawl. "*Anda, preciosa!*" he calls out. Walk, my precious! Then he tosses off *piropos*, little words of flattery. "With every step you take, *mi vida,* flowers spring up from the earth." Or, "If beauty were a sin, *mi amor,* you would spend your life in confession." Or, "*Ay angelita,* you have so many curves, and I have no brakes." He does have brakes, of course, and slams on them whenever he spies a micromini skirt.

"Wow!" he says to me. "Did you see that? That is poetry, man. Living poetry."

Fat women in particular are singled out for flattery: "I have so little time, and you offer so much to love."

He tells me, "It's good to make the fat ones happy. They need much loving."

When it comes to dispensing *piropos,* Fredo never discriminates against age, color, or size. He feels it is his solemn duty to let every woman know that she is the most beautiful, most desirable woman on earth. The women seem to take it all in stride. I'm sure they hear *piropos* from many Puerto Rican males. But now and then one will smile in appreciation, and Fredo will beam with delight. Life is good.

To drive with Fredo is to experience firsthand the twin forces that rule the island: Love and Anarchy. It's been ever thus. In *The Puerto Ricans: A Documentary History,* Kal Wagenheim and Olga Jimenez de Wagenheim tell of a bishop from Spain who visited in the eighteenth century and observed that

> there is no order at all. . . . the entire population of the town seems to be on horseback, riding frantically in every direction. Despite the confusion, there is rarely an accident, and if there is, the victim is usually some Spaniard who has turned the corner and, faced by a platoon of riders, cannot avoid the horses with the same skill as the *criollos.* Even when the horse is racing full speed, the *criollos* leave the reins loose upon the saddle, cross their arms, and while smoking a cigar, voice their compliments to the ladies in the windows.

The *criollos*—creoles—were the islanders. They included the native-born whites who owned the large sugar plantations and cattle ranches; the mulattos, mostly small farmers; and the Afro-Caribbeans, the escaped slaves and free blacks who lived in villages by the sea and harvested fish, crabs and oysters.

The white Europeans were called *hombres de la otra banda.* These "men of the other band" were the governing elite, from the military, the Roman Catholic Church, and the wealthy Spanish merchant class. They looked down upon the native-born creoles, no matter their shade.

Not long after Puerto Rico was discovered, it became an afterthought in the great colonial scheme of things. Spain controlled all commerce and immigration, and the result for Puerto Rico was little commerce and no immigration. Still, the island's population grew at a surprising rate, the result of a rather astonishing fecundity. This was aided no doubt by a complete lack of inhibitions when it came to premarital, nonmarital, and interracial sex.

From the very beginning, the Spaniards were smitten by the native Indian women. "They appear a friendly and amiable race," wrote Columbus. "Well-made with fine shapes and faces, tawny skin. Their eyes are large and very beautiful. Their discourse is ever sweet and gentle and always accompanied with a smile."

His fellow countrymen were struck by the sight of "sweet smelling maidens" who bathed many times a day.

For the Taínos, the tradition of formal marriage did not exist. The conquistadors took this as a license to take a number of Indian women as their mistresses; some claimed as many as five. When word of this practice reached Spain, there was much official consternation. To the King, it was a breach of knightly etiquette; to the Church, it was a mortal sin. Cardinal Cisneros dispatched three Hieronymite monks to the New World to warn the conquistadors they must marry their Indian mistresses or suffer the fires of hell. But the cardinal's words were largely ignored, the men preferring their heaven on earth.

Only a generation after Puerto Rico's discovery, there were more people of mixed race on the island than there were pure whites and pure Indians. When Africans entered the mix, yet another "race" was created. To make sense of it all, royal officials in Spain listed the origins of no less than sixteen castes of color: Spaniard and Indian beget *mestizo*. *Mestizo* and Spaniard beget *castizo*. Spaniard and Negro beget *mulato*. Spaniard and *mulato* beget *morisco.* And so on, defining *albinos, lobos, zam-baigos, cambujos, albarazados, barcinos, coyotes, chamisos*—until one arrives at the ultimate expression of miscegenation: *ahí te estás,* "there you have it"—or, who knows what!

These forbidden couplings continued to distress the Catholic bishops throughout the colonial period. They sent Spanish priests into the villages to warn the creoles about the evils of fornication and miscegenation. The villagers—white, black, and mulatto—would celebrate the priest's arrival with a communal rosary. This was soon followed by endless rounds of cockfights, horse races, and parties.

The favorite diversion was dancing. When someone gave a dance, hundreds of people came from everywhere. No invitation required. The villagers would dance around roaring bonfires to the music of timbrels, gourds, maracas, and guitars. Then they would slip off into the night and fornicate and miscegenate until dawn. The priests often took part in the festivities—much to the bishop's chagrin.

In 1898, despite almost four hundred years of clerical finger wagging, one out of three children in Puerto Rico was born out of wedlock. The new colonial rulers, the Americans, were appalled.

The appointed governor, Charles Allen, sent out a fact-finding commission, which reported, "They live so close to nature that things which seem improper to us are the innocent affairs of their daily lives. They are naked and not ashamed. They are married and not parsoned. The system is strange, but it answers."

As Fredo cruises through a red traffic light in one of San Juan's busiest intersections, he spies a doddering old crone on the corner. He immediately hits the brakes to offer her a *piropo.* "If I were a submarine, I'd dive to the deepest depths of your heart."

Then, turning to me, he says, "Now she feels young again. Why should no one love them because they are old?"

The system is strange, but it answers.

CHAPTER 5
Jurutungo

A person should swallow a toad every morning to be sure of not meeting with anything more revolting in the day ahead.
—Nicolas Chamfort

Our research vessel is just a few weeks away from delivery, and we're still in need of much gear to outfit it. Fear and anxiety have determined my priorities: life jackets, life rings, life raft. An abandon-boat kit with bottled water, fish hooks, waterproof matches, cans of Spam, red beans, and fruit cocktail—the latter to prevent scurvy. A first aid kit with iodine, sunburn cream, morphine, and bandages. Flashlights and spotlights, foghorns and whistles, smoke canisters and signal guns. A lead line for when the depth sounder goes haywire. A distress flag for when the radio fails. A paddle for when the engine craps out. And most important, smoke signals and emergency flares.

"These things look cool, man," says Fredo, loading a case of red parachute flares into the wagon. "I really hope we get to use them."

"No, Fredo, you don't. It's not a good thing if we ever have to use them."

"I mean like in a test, you know. We have to test them, *verdad?* Or one day we are out there in the ocean and the boat is sinking and here comes a rescue plane and we don't know how to use these things. Then sharks start chewing on the boat and—"

"OK, Fredo, OK! We'll test one of each."

"Yah, mon!"

Fredo knows just the place to fire them off: a secluded cove in Piñones, an undeveloped stretch of beaches, coves, mangroves, and lagoons just east of San Juan. The dirt road that leads through it is dotted with crudely built shacks and fast-food kiosks. They offer deep-fried snapper, deep-fried salt cod, deep-fried fingers of cornmeal, and deep-fried plantains, ripe or green. They're cooked in half-barrels filled with oil and stoked with burning driftwood. Smoke from sizzling food, salty wood, and cooking oil wafts through the air and stirs the appetite. This is not where you go to flush your arteries.

The community here is predominantly black, which is unusual on the island. In most places, the local population is quite mixed. But the people here in Piñones are descended from slaves who escaped from plantations centuries ago. For much of its history, Puerto Rico was a haven for runaway slaves, especially from other Caribbean islands. The harboring of fugitives rankled the Spanish ruling class, and strict laws were passed to prevent it—with the usual effect. Once, when an escaped slave was captured in a coastal village, it was found that more than twenty creole families had provided him with a safe haven at one time or another. Other laws were passed forbidding fraternization between owners and slaves—again, with the usual effect. The creole farmers often played cards with their slaves and even partied with them, dancing until the cock crowed.

Until the sugar boom of the nineteenth century and the influx of South American royalists, slavery was not an important component of the island's economy. Even at slavery's peak, slaves never comprised more than 14 percent of the population. The creoles granted freedom to most of them long before the institution was officially ended. And it was Puerto Rican slaveholders who traveled to Spain to argue for its abolition.

When Fredo and I arrive in Piñones, many of the kiosks are closed. They generally come alive on weekends when *sanjuaneros* flock here to eat, drink, and gossip under the whispery Australian pines. But we do come upon an open kiosk where Fredo knows the vendor. She's an old black woman named Doña Rosa, who sports a T-shirt with a picture of a smiling tree frog.

Fredo tells her that she looks lovely today and that her red kerchief brings out the pink in her cheeks. Doña Rosa waves him off with a laugh: "*Gallito!*" Little rooster.

We order some codfish fritters and beers, and Doña Rosa tells us about an army of land crabs that marched right through the front door of her shack just when, by the grace of God, she had a big pot boiling, and as they marched in she scooped

them up and tossed them into the pot. Now she has a mountain of turnovers stuffed with land crab and Fredo must take
some with him. But no, *gallito,* she tells him, she won't take any
money for them. They are just for him to enjoy. Him and the
skinny little gringo who should eat more Puerto Rican food because he's a bag of bones. She wraps the *pastelillos* in newspaper
and the grease quickly bleeds through. Fredo discreetly slips a
few bills under the counter mat. We bid Doña Rosa farewell
and continue on down the road.

To our left are high dunes that lead down to the sea. Few
people swim here. It's too risky. There are fossilized corals that
can scrape your skin, swirling eddies that can dash you against
rocks, and fierce riptides that can carry you out to sea.

To the right are pine woods with makeshift shacks scattered here and there. The dwellings are constructed of weathered planks and driftwood, with roofs made of palm fronds.
Most look as if they were thrown together yesterday, and perhaps many were. When storms strike the northern coast during
flood tide, the high waters surge across Piñones, spiriting away
coconuts and logs and little shacks. No matter. When the waters recede, new homes are put up in a day or two.

We turn off the dirt road and follow tire tracks in the sand.
Signs warn against trespassing.

"They don't really mean it," says Fredo.

We come to a beach where another sign warns that no vehicles are allowed.

"People drive here all the time," says Fredo.

We park the wagon next to a sign that says there's no parking.

"It's OK," says Fredo, "Everyone parks here. On the weekend there's a line of cars a mile long."

We carry a box of combustibles to the water's edge, and we break open a case of parachute flares that's labeled, "For Emergency Use Only."

"I bet everybody tests these things first, right?" Fredo says. He takes out a cylinder the size of a Pringles can and pops off the cap.

"Point it out to sea, Fredo."

"OK, man. Out to sea she goes."

He pulls out the safety pin. Squeezes the plastic trigger. And *whhhooosh!* A rocket shoots into the sky and at the zenith of its trajectory—*whhhooooof*—a parachute opens and slowly descends to the sea, shooting red sparks all the way down.

"*Viva la revolución!*" shouts Fredo the Anarchist.

If during the colonial era the island had two economies, the official and the contraband, it also had two political faces, one that paid lip service to the edicts from Spain and another that followed its own laws and customs. This explains much of the apparent fickleness in the loyalties of the creoles to the various regimes of Spain.

In 1820, when the Spanish Army revolted, King Ferdinand VII was forced to accept a constitutional monarchy. In Puerto Rico there were joyous gatherings with festive lights and eloquent speeches celebrating the new Constitution. Three years later, when absolute monarchy was restored and the Constitution abolished, there were joyous gatherings with festive lights and eloquent speeches celebrating the return of the King. A decade later, when royalty was again given the boot, Puerto

Ricans again had reason to party. And why not? What did it matter what went on in Spain? The result was always the same for the island: a new set of rules to disobey. And that was certainly worth a fiesta.

When the Americans invaded in 1898 they, too, were surprised and heartened by the reception. "The American forces that landed in Porto Rico, were supposed to be invading a hostile territory," wrote Richard Harding Davis, a war correspondent. Instead, the people "received our troops with one hand open and the other presenting either a bouquet, or a bottle. Our troops clasped both hands."

Later, General Nelson Miles issued a proclamation to "the inhabitants of Porto Rico": "This is not a war of devastation, but one to give all . . . the advantages and blessings of an enlightened civilization." The people cheered his words with gusto. Anarchy is dead! Long live anarchy!

The testing of our emergency flares has proved so invaluable that we've gone through both a case of flares and a six-pack of India beer while shooting them off. Now, with the sun dipping low in the sky, we take a stroll up the deserted beach to pick up spent flares. The ocean is very calm, like a turquoise lake, and there's not a whisper of wind. Slack tide reveals long stretches of pocked coral rock. Bowls the size of hot tubs have been carved into the rock, and tiny crabs and minnows dart about in pools. Inshore are mounds of shells. We pick through the shells and find what appear to be pottery shards. I realize this must be an ancient midden: a congealed mound of shells, charcoal chunks, animal bones, and pottery shards. One would have thought that centuries of tidal action would have carried the remains out to sea. But they're still here. And they've been here for more than five centuries.

The Taíno Indians were a seafaring people who not only fished the waters but traveled far and wide by sea, trading with their fellow tribesmen on Hispaniola and Cuba to the west and the Virgin Islands to the east. Our word "canoe" comes from the Taíno word *canoa*. The Indians were skilled navigators and fearless sailors. Columbus was often astonished to see a lone Taíno paddling far out at sea.

"Some of these boats are large, some small, some of medium size," wrote Columbus. "Yet they row many of the larger rowboats with eighteen cross-benches, with which they cross to all those Islands, which are innumerable, and with these feats they perform their trading, and carry commerce on them. I saw some of these canoes which were carrying seventy and eighty rowers."

These larger canoes were owned by the chiefs and could carry more than a hundred people. Imagine all those men, women, and children, with their bundles of cassava roots and sweet potatoes and dried iguanas, paddling off to visit distant islands. Passengers on the first cruise ships in the Caribbean.

Each canoe was made from a single log of the silk-cotton tree. Not only was it a fine hardwood, but a powerful spirit lived within it. Before a silk-cotton tree could be felled, the shaman would have to ask permission from the spirit of the tree. To communicate with the spirit he would smoke cohoba and put himself in a trance. Then he'd dance around the tree, singing and shaking a rattle. The spirit of the tree would tell the priest what shape the canoe should take, what length it should be, and what carvings would decorate its hull. When the canoe had been built according to the spirit's demands, the spirit would enter it.

Fredo hands me a small pottery shard. "Take it. They're for good luck." It occurs to me that we might be removing artifacts from an archaeological site. What if everyone raided the midden for souvenirs?

"Take it, *Capitán*," Fredo insists. "Everybody takes one." So I pocket the shard. You can't have too much good luck.

"You know, Fredo. I've been thinking about giving the boat an Indian name. A Taíno Indian name. I'm thinking of calling the boat *Maroho*. After the Taíno god of fair weather."

He looks at me with a blank expression. His eyes blink with distinct squeezes of the lids.

"You hate the name," I say.

"No, I like it. I like it."

But I can tell he doesn't.

"It just sounds a little like *carajo*," he says. "You know, like *vete pa'l carajo!* Go to hell!"

"Yes, Fredo, I know what *carajo* means. But the boat's name is *Maroho*. Ma-ro-ho. You have to give it a kind of poetic inflection."

"*Maroho*," says Fredo, trying it on for size. "Ma-RO-ho. MAROHO! OK. That works for me. I like it."

Most of the flares parachuted down into the sea and are now drifting out with the tide. A few of them were carried by the wind toward a promontory on the other side of the cove. I decide to hike out there and pick up whatever spent flares I can find. Fredo will stay behind to keep an eye on our vehicle. The tradition of plunder and pillage is still alive and well in Puerto Rico.

The promontory is overgrown with a dense tangle of vegetation. I forge my way through a tunnel of twisted trees. Dead leaves carpet the narrow trail like lightly browned pancakes. Countless lizards scurry away, rustling the leaves with a spooky patter. Here and there, massive reddish-brown termite mounds cling to trees. There are also swarms of mosquitoes, which remind me to add insect repellent to the boat's emergency kit. I spot a spent flare in a sea almond tree, the chute stuck in a branch with the flare dangling below it like some hapless parachutist. There's an enormous green lizard between me and the tree. It's about four feet long. It flicks his tongue at me then slinks off. I quickly retrieve the flare.

On the promontory's rocky outcrop, the fossilized coral has formed a carpet of black daggers that point upward. Stepping very carefully, I find a few more flares between cracks in the rocks. Long, low swells roll in, perhaps from a passing ship. The swells wash over a mesa of coral and smash against the rocks, thoroughly soaking me. Wiping salt water from my face, I see a couple of other flares floating just offshore where a submerged barrier reef meets the open sea. Far out on the horizon, something else catches my eye.

It's a ship, a big ship steaming east. I shield my eyes from the sun for a better look. It's riding high in the water, which leads me to believe that it's a container ship. But the ship is moving very fast, and now, as it draws closer, I can see it's huge. In fact, it's an aircraft carrier. Now other ships come into view. The carrier is like a fat mother goose gliding across a pond with

her goslings. Her goslings are missile cruisers and destroyers
and radar pickets and attack submarines. I count a half dozen
of them, and there are probably an equal number beyond the
horizon.

I haven't seen a fleet of ships like this since Vietnam. There,
the Seventh Fleet prowled the coastal waters. Its mission was to
provide support to shore-based operations through naval gunnery bombardment. I remember watching the Fleet at work
from the bridge of the SS *Beaver Victory.* Spotter planes helped
the ships' gunnery crews home in on their targets. Then the
cruisers let the big guns rip. The vibrations from the gunfire
shook the air, rattling my teeth from miles away. You could
hear loud *KA-FWOOMs* and see huge balls of white and orange smoke spewing out of the gun muzzles. The ocean was
flattened in the direction they were firing. And where were
those monster projectiles headed? I could visualize their targets:
Vietnamese peasants in straw hats and pajamas and bare feet,
scurrying around trying to take cover.

Vietnam is particularly vulnerable to naval gunnery. It's
a narrow country with a two-thousand-mile coastline. Many
populated areas lie close to the sea and are within firing range
of the big ships. Ships on the "gun line" can destroy supply
depots and ammunition dumps and even entire companies of
enemy troops. A whole village can be obliterated in the blink of
an eye. Now and then that would happen, the most notorious
instance being Ben Tre, a friendly village near Saigon, that was
leveled by errant missiles. Afterward, assessing the damage, the
US officer in charge uttered the infamous words, "We had to
destroy the village in order to save it."

The sight of so many warships so far from the war zone gives me chills. It's as if they've come from *Jurutungo,* Puerto Rican slang for the middle of nowhere.

Where are they bound?

CHAPTER 6
The Governor Gets the Ass

Some got shot and some got drowned
And some beyond the seas
Got scraped to death with oyster shells
Among the Caribbees.
                    —the Ghost of Nell Cook

I hear it first from my brother-in-law Adaír. We're knocking down cold Indias in Pepe's Place, a neighborhood bar with a jukebox that features lots of *salsa* and a single George Harrison disc, "My Sweet Lord," which Pepe has added just for me. Adaír's *amigos* and *amigas* are here, among them Wilfredo, a lanky slow-witted young man with a dog named Puppy; Ramón, an aspiring *salsa* trumpeter who sells used cars for a living; and Blanquita, a mannish woman who punctuates every sentence with a strident *exacto!*

Adaír gives a delighted cackle. "So did you hear? The governor got the ass, man. Hahahahaaa! He really got the ass!"

Adaír is no fan of Governor Ferré, who is pro-statehood while Adaír is staunchly for independence. Adaír's political views emerged after he returned to the US from Vietnam with shrapnel in his chest and Agent Orange in his lungs. He was re-stationed at Fort Benning, Georgia, where he soon learned that in stateside America he was just another person of color.

"Puerto Ricans go to Vietnam! Risk their lives!" he once railed to me. "And then those racist mutha fuggas treat us like *mierda!* Like shit! To hell with them. And the 'statehooders,' too." To Adaír, the governor is a man without pride.

"You should see Ferré now. *Cabrón!* He got the ass, man. Hahahaha. He really got the ass." Cheers all around in Pepe's Place.

"He had it coming," says Ramón.

"*Exacto!*" says Blanquita.

The incident occurred while Governor Ferré was visiting the little island of Culebra. Twenty miles northeast of the main island of Puerto Rico, it is the second largest of the Spanish Virgin Islands and is often called the Last Virgin because it is the westernmost in the chain. The Navy has been shelling the place for almost thirty years, much to the distress of the 743 Puerto Ricans who call it home. Now, to the Culebrans' shock, the Navy wants to expand the target range and use heavier missiles—hence the arrival of the big ships from Jurutungo.

In mainland Puerto Rico, the problems of the offshore islanders usually draw little notice; the passages that separate the islands from the mainland might as well be an ocean wide. So when Governor Ferré visited Culebra to meet with its residents and hear their concerns, he got an earful. The Culebrans told him stories about what they endure during the bombing runs—quaking homes and schoolhouses, trauma from being constantly under siege, even miscarriages induced by the concussive shelling. They spoke of mass killings of fish, of the destruction of coral reefs, and of a land so rife with unexploded ordnance that a casual stroll in the countryside could prove fatal.

Ferré decided to circle Culebra in his private yacht to assess firsthand the damage from the shelling. He was cruising by Flamenco Beach, a prime nesting site for sea turtles and a favorite target of the Navy, when without warning a Navy gunnery crew opened fire. Rocket mortars screamed over the governor's head; others struck the water just off a beach where children were playing. Fortunately the gunners' aims were off, and no one was hurt. But the incident sent shock waves of anger across Puerto Rico and raised awareness of the serious issues facing Culebrans.

The idea that the small inhabited island of Culebra would be used for target practice can be traced all the way back to the nineteenth century and the lectures of Alfred Thayer Mahan, a graduate of the US Naval Academy and Captain of the USS *Pocahontas* during the American Civil War. Captain Mahan was a rather feckless skipper with the dangerous habits of running his ship aground and colliding with other vessels. He was better suited to writing histories about wars than actually participating in them.

His first book, *The Influence of Sea Power Upon History, 1660-1783,* was published in 1872. In it, he argued the importance of sea power to empire building, and the book was eagerly devoured by a young politician named Theodore Roosevelt. Roosevelt often attended Mahan's lectures. The old captain would expound upon the virtues of Manifest Destiny and the key to its realization: the acquisition by the United States of islands that could serve as naval stations for battleships and cruisers. Mahan spoke of Puerto Rico as a place that could serve as a gatekeeper to the Caribbean Sea.

In 1898, during the closing days of the Spanish-American War, Roosevelt wrote in a letter to his close friend Senator Henry Cabot Lodge, "Give my best love to Nannie and do not make peace until we get Porto Rico." To which Lodge replied, "Porto Rico is not forgotten and we mean to have it." By year's end they had it.

In 1906 Theodore Roosevelt became the first US president to visit Puerto Rico. "The scenery is wonderfully beautiful," he wrote, "especially among the mountains of the interior, which constitute a veritable tropical Switzerland." An avid birdwatcher, Roosevelt was particularly impressed by the island of Culebra, with its royal terns, sandwich terns, and bridled terns; its brown, red-footed, and masked boobies; its laughing gulls, tropicbirds and mangrove cuckoos. In 1909, he designated Culebra one of the America's first national wildlife refuges. Paradoxically, he also established on the island the Culebra Naval Reservation. This would be the first step in the slow, steady encroachment of the military on Puerto Rico's private lands.

In 1916, on the cusp of the United States' entrance into World War I, a 300-acre tract of land in the suburbs of San Juan was appropriated as a training area for army maneuvers. It was named Fort Buchanan. Gradually the fort expanded to 1,500 acres and then, during World War II, to 4,500 acres, three times the size of New York's Central Park. And this in the most crowded city in the Caribbean.

In 1939 the Army Air Corps expropriated 3,800 acres of prime beachfront property on the northwest coast of Puerto Rico for the Borinquen Army Air Field. It soon earned a dubious reputation as the site of the infamous "Battle of Borinquen Field," when nervous guards opened machine-gun fire on an "invasion force" that consisted of a friendly merchant ship that had drifted too close to shore.

A year later, Naval Air Station Isla Grande was established on a tiny island in San Juan Bay. To service the young American flyboys, a collection of whorehouses, strip clubs, and rum joints sprang up in the environs like so many fungi. These establishments were especially prevalent in Miramar, once one of the loveliest and most elegant old neighborhoods in San Juan.

Another major land grab took place on the easternmost edge of Puerto Rico. This time it was for the Roosevelt Roads Naval Station. At more than 8,000 acres, "Roady" would become the largest military complex in the Caribbean, with seven thousand personnel, a hundred miles of paved road, and thirteen hundred buildings, as well as the requisite swimming pools, bowling alleys, golf courses, and riding stables. It is a military enclave with little or no interaction with the people, customs, or environment beyond its gates. The only indication that it is in Puerto Rico is the name of the outdoor movie theater. It's called "The Coquí," after the tree frogs that chirp loudly and incessantly through movies like *The Green Berets,* during which they've been known to drown out John Wayne barking, "Out here, due process is a bullet." *Coh-kee coh-kee coh-kee!*

The amount of arable land in Puerto Rico that has been expropriated by the armed forces is astonishing. If Puerto Rico were the size of the continental US, it would be as if all the farmland east of the Mississippi had been confiscated for military purposes. Other seized lands include prime waterfront property with virgin beaches and secluded bays and unspoiled surroundings—well-suited for nature reserves or the burgeoning ecotourism industry yet off-limits to all Puerto Ricans.

But it is the outer islands, the Spanish Virgins, that have suffered most from these land grabs. Vieques, the largest island, is a land of gentle hills and lush valleys, with a stunning bioluminescent bay. In 1941, 22,000 acres—two thirds of Vieques—were confiscated. Most of its three thousand inhabitants were deported. They were given thirty dollars for their homes and twenty-four hours to be gone. Only the very center of the island still belongs to the locals. "So we feel like a sandwich," one resident says.

Now it is Culebra, the Last Virgin, that the Navy gazes upon with hungry eyes. The island is roughly four by seven miles and shaped like an ocean sunfish with a large forked tail, a mola mola swimming east. At the time of the American takeover in 1898, there were some six hundred residents on Culebra. They eked out a living catching fish and turtles, raising cattle and goats, planting pumpkins and plantains. The island had forty-five houses, one church, a government house, a pier, and a lone settlement, San Ildefonso. With the creation of a US Naval station in 1901, the residents were moved to a new town center named Dewey, after the naval hero of the Spanish American War. It was Commodore George Dewey who famously uttered, "You may fire when you are ready, Gridley."

For the next forty years, there was a peaceful coexistence between the residents and the military. Then, in 1941, came Executive Order 8684. Signed by Franklin D. Roosevelt, the emergency decree authorized the use of the Culebra for target practice by the military. A third of Culebra was confiscated; residents were evicted from their properties. Bull's-eyes were set up in the hills on the north side of Culebra. Throughout World War II, the island quivered and shook under the relentless shelling. And there were accidents: one Culebran lost his right arm, another lost his left, and yet another lost his life. All from picking up unexploded ordnance.

The end of the wartime emergency brought no peace to the Culebrans. The shelling continued. And now, twenty-nine years after Executive Order 8684, shelling is about to intensify. With the war escalating in Vietnam, the military has developed a new class of weapons designed to carry heavier warheads over longer ranges. These missiles need to be tested. And what better place than Culebra? A useless clump of coral and scrub. A no-man's-land of mosquitoes, lizards, and birds with names like mangrove cuckoo. True, Culebra is inhabited. But to the military, there is a tried-and-true solution. Relocate the Culebrans.

Of course, the Culebrans would need to be compensated, but since their average annual income is four hundred dollars, how much could *that* cost? As for Culebra's industry, there is but one: a small factory that breeds bacteria-free laboratory rats. No problem. Send people and rats to the mainland. And fire when ready, Gridley!

It's a simple plan, yes, but one that is not proving easy to execute. Apparently, no one in the Department of Defense has read *The Mouse That Roared*. And roaring loudest is Culebra's mayor, Ramón Feliciano. Feliciano is a dark, slender man, an unimposing figure in an oversized blue suit and a schoolboy tie. He's soft-spoken and polite, even shy. It's easy to underestimate his intellect, his courage, and his tenacity.

He was raised in a family of subsistence farmers on the north coast of Culebra. It was an idyllic country childhood. But the Felicianos were among the approximately forty families evicted by the US Navy in 1944. Their sprawling wood house overlooking Flamenco Bay would become a target. They managed to find a place to live near Dewey, but many others—about a thousand of Culebra's fifteen hundred residents, by war's end—were forced to leave the island. Most moved to the Puerto Rican mainland or to the Virgin Islands or to New York, Chicago, or Philadelphia. The Felicianos bid adiós to uncles and aunts and cousins and neighbors—a close-knit community that had called Culebra home for generations. The ties of families and friends were forever broken.

The memory of this forced relocation has instilled in the young mayor a determination to prevent history from repeating itself. When word of the Navy's new eviction plans leaked out, Feliciano called for an emergency town meeting. Fishers, farmers, and rat-factory workers gathered in the tiny colonial-era mayor's office to hear him speak.

"The Navy wants to strangle us," he said, "and force us to leave. They found it easy to take our land in the past. I say to you, make life impossible for them. Use every means possible to rescue your land!"

Feliciano called for a vote. It would be on whether *the Navy itself* should be evicted. It was a bold motion, ingenious even, for it would shift the debate. In a show of hands, the citizens of the municipality of Culebra in the Free Associated State of Puerto Rico voted the Navy off their island.

Somehow the US press got wind of this quixotic gesture. A spate of articles have appeared in the *Washington Post* and the *New York Times*. Who are these Culebrans and why is the US Navy shelling their island? they ask. There is a growing chorus of disapproval of the Navy's plans for Culebra. Newspaper editorials and television news reports are playing up the David-versus-Goliath angle. Even US congressmen are questioning the military's very presence on the island.

All this controversy presents a quandary to Governor Ferré. Ferré is something of a Renaissance man. He is an MIT graduate with a degree in engineering, and he has made a fortune in the cement business. He is also a gifted classical pianist, a stalwart patron of the arts, and an eloquent writer, as illustrated by his words on a plaque in Ponce:

Dónde hay emoción, hay arte
Dónde hay arte, hay vida

Dónde hay vida, hay esperanza
Dónde hay esperanza, hay redención.

Where there is emotion, he writes, there is art. Where there is art, there is life. Where there is life, there is hope. Where there is hope, there is redemption.

Luis Ferré sees Puerto Rican statehood as the only path to first-class citizenship. But he broke away from the Republican (pro-statehood) party and campaigned for governor as a pro-statehood independent. He won a surprise victory in the election, ending two decades of rule by the Popular Democratic Party—the *populares* who favor Commonwealth. Still, his hold on power is very tenuous. The Governor's fate could very well be determined by his response to the crisis on Culebra. His pro-statehood party has worked hard to persuade Puerto Ricans that the Mother Country is a bastion of freedom, with a government of the people, by the people, and for the people; dedicated to the proposition that all men are created equal; and committed to the inalienable rights of life, liberty, and the pursuit of happiness—in short, a country worthy of joining as a full-fledged state. To admit that the US is ignoring these principles in Culebra would make statehood a difficult sell.

A few weeks ago, the governor decided to take a more proactive stance. He would be the bridge over troubled waters between the Navy and Culebra's citizens. Hence his ill-fated trip to the island and the ensuing humiliation of having to dodge mortar fire at the hands of trigger-happy swabbies.

Governor Luis A. Ferré still believes in Winston Churchill's maxim: "You can always rely on America to do the right thing—

after it has tried every other option." But what is the right thing for Culebra? And how can America be directed toward it? Ferré mulls these questions behind closed doors in La Fortaleza, the governor's palace. No one is privy to his thinking.

Ever since the governor "got the ass," nothing is quite the same around the office. Something is stirring. Furtive whispers. Secret meetings. An electric undercurrent. Charged. Ready to snap, crackle, and pop. The governor, it seems, has been asking questions about the research capabilities of the Area of Natural Resources. And about its new vessel, the R/V *Maroho*.

CHAPTER 7
Yesterday

You taught me language,
and my profit on't is
I know how to curse.
— Caliban to Prospero, *The Tempest*

"**C**apitán. How is the boat coming along?" Cruz-Cruz is not his usual ebullient self; he is Lt. Col. Cruz-Cruz, Military Man on a Mission.

Ever since I've been here, not one person in the Area of Natural Resources has asked me about the boat. Nor has anyone felt inclined to pay its captain. Once a day, I go to Payroll and Disbursements, where Delila, an enormous woman with bleached blonde hair streaked with chartreuse, holds court. She sits behind enormous stacks of paperwork, busily painting her fingernails cerulean blue and chatting away with the other women in the office about the latest twists and turns of

Simplemente María, a Peruvian soap opera, or *novella,* as they're called. María was a poor country girl, a housemaid, who was knocked up by a caddish businessman. Still, she managed to pull herself up by her bootstraps with the help of her literacy teacher, the patient and virtuous Maestro Esteban. For twenty years—for 225 episodes—Maestro Esteban has secretly loved María. And now at last he's proposed to her.

"But she afrai' to marry with him," rues Delila. "And after he save her, he *save* her, *coño!*"

My own salvation—the form that authorizes my paycheck—lies at the bottom of a stack. But it never seems to move upward to where it might be approved and signed by Delila. Nor have I been reimbursed for the assorted equipment and charts purchased with my own dwindling funds; that form lies near the bottom of yet another stack. When I bring this to Delila's attention, she looks at me with a stunned, even hurt expression. It's a look that says, How could you even bring up such trivial matters when María's wedding to Maestro Esteban could fall apart at any moment!

I go back to my wall-less, phone-less, desk-less office defeated and demoralized. Were it not for the generosity of *la familia Ríos,* my own family would be living in some rickety shack in Barrio Cantera, surviving on food stamps and defecating in the Martín Peña Canal.

And I'm not the only one who isn't getting paid. Nauticenter, the marine supply house, has yet to receive a penny for the anchors, line, and safety gear we purchased months ago.

"*Mierda!*" shouts Natividad, the owner, wiping the seat of his pants with the purchase order I've just given him. "You take this paper, *Capitán,* and tell Governor Luis A. Ferré to wipe his *culo* with it."

My daily trip to the boatyard continues to produce the usual results. Frustration. Fulmination. Exasperation. The hull sits on its cradle, the cabin and the main deck on their respective sawhorses; never the three shall meet. The engine arrived weeks ago, a 200-HP Chrysler Marine inboard and its Volvo outboard stern drive. Both sit in their crates. The reason time exists, said Albert Einstein, is so that everything doesn't happen at once. No fear of that here.

"Don't worry, *Capitán,*" says Bruno the foreman, "we are right on schedule. A little wiring, a little plumbing, some mechanical work . . . and we are ready to go!"

"So where are the people performing these tasks? Where is the electrician? Where is the plumber? Where is the mechanic? And please don't tell me it's a holiday."

"You just miss them. They went to get the things they need. And by the way we have still not received payment for the extras."

"The extras?"

"*Sí.* The portholes and the windows and the guard rails and the cabin roof and the toilet and the—"

"Those are *extras?*"

He shrugs. "*Sí.* Extras."

I explain all this to Cruz-Cruz, but it falls on deaf ears.

"*Capitán,*" he says, "we need the boat yesterday."

"Yesterday."

"*Sí.* Yesterday."

"I can't get anything done today, sir. I can't even get anything done tomorrow. I doubt I can get anything done yesterday."

"*Por favor,*" pleads Cruz-Cruz, "we need the boat to be ready."

"Can you tell me what's going on?" I ask. "Is there something I should know?"

"Yesterday," he says. "Please."

"Let us walk," says Gabriel Ferrer. Gabriel is the architect *cum* philosopher for the Area of Natural Resources who interviewed me for the job. He's become a good friend. I assume that his suggestion to take a walk means he has something to confide in me about the boat.

"So, Gabo, this new sense of urgency," I say as we stroll the Plaza de Armas. "What's going on?"

Gabriel often speaks in parables, which makes it difficult to get a straight answer out of him. "The lion may lay down with the lamb," he says, "but that does not assure the lamb a good night's sleep." He gives me a look that says, Do you catch my drift? I nod—though I don't.

I visit the office of Ambrosio Freyre, the geologist with a penchant for dirty jokes. When I ask him about the sudden need for the boat to be ready, he rises from his desk and closes the door. Then he speaks *sotto voce.* "Have you heard the one about the *gringo turista* traveling in Spain?"

"No sir, I haven't."

"So this *turista,* he goes into a restaurant and he orders *la especialidad de la casa,* the specialty of the house. The waiter brings out *papas,* vegetables, and two big pieces of meat.

"'What is this meat?' asks the *gringo.*

"'*Cojones,* señor,' says the waiter.

"'But what are *cojones?*'

"'They are testicles. These *cojones* are from the bull who lost in the *plaza de toro* today. It is a tradition to eat those of the loser.'

"At first, the *gringo* is disgusted, but then he decides, *bueno,* he is on vacation; he should be a little adventurous. So he eats them. And to his amazement he finds them quite delicious. The next day he returns to the restaurant and straight away he orders the *cojones.* They, too, are delicious, but he is somewhat disappointed.

"'The ones I had yesterday were much bigger,' he says. 'Are you sure these are *cojones?*'

"'*Ah sí, señor,*' says the waiter. 'But it is not always the bull who loses in the ring.'"

Back in my wall-less, phone-less, desk-less office, I vent to Fredo. "I just can't believe it. The boat should be ready—needs to be ready—by now. And they're not doing squat over in the boatyard."

"Let me talk to Bruno," says Fredo.

"I've talked to him, Fredo. I've begged him, pleaded with him every way I know how."

"*Capitán.* Let me talk to him. *Se necesita un ratón pa' coger un ratón.*" It takes a mouse to catch a mouse.

Hours later, Fredo comes back from the boatyard beaming with triumph. "The boat will be ready in one week."

"Hah!"

"*De veras!* Really. They have promised. And they will do it. They will finish the boat in one week."

"Hah!"

"I told them the governor has a very important mission for us. And we need the boat. For Puerto Rico. For our country. *Por la patria!*"

"And that worked?"

"No. They laughed. So that's when I told them about the fiesta."

"What fiesta?"

"The fiesta we are going to have when the boat is finished."

"Jesus, Fredo."

"The fiesta with rum, music, and those hot little *chiquitas* in miniskirts who work in the office. I invited Bruno. He now says the boat will be ready in one week. He swears on his life. I believe him. The boat will be ready."

And it is. Well, in two weeks really. Which is one week on Puerto Rican time. And here is our little boat now, poised in midair and swinging in its sling, a Felliniesque vision in pink and orange. The crane sets it gently down on the trailer. We strap the boat securely in place and, with Fredo behind the wheel, tow the R/V *Maroho* out of its cavernous womb and into the bright light of day.

The public ramp at Isla Grande is about an hour away in the midday traffic. It's going to be a nerve-racking hour with

Fredo driving, the boat and trailer careening this way and that and almost sideswiping vehicles, street signs, and pedestrians.

In Miramar we drive past the Kit-Kat Klub, the Black Angus, and the Escudo Bar. Painted ladies gawk at the garishly colored boat. It looks like a pimpmobile. Fredo tosses them *piropos:* "We go to sea, my precious, to bring you pearls as beautiful as your eyes."

On Isla Grande we tow the boat past the Coast Guard station to the boat ramp on San Juan Bay. Already our coworkers from the Area of Natural Resources have gathered here to celebrate our maiden voyage. Cruz-Cruz circulates among the well-wishers like a proud papa giving away his daughter at a wedding. Gabriel is here, as are Ambrosio and Mercedes. Delila is here too, and she looks greatly relieved. Apparently the wedding of Maestro Esteban to María, on *Simplemente María,* went off without a hitch. By all accounts the filming of the wedding scene was a spectacular event. Some ten thousand people crowded outside a church in Lima, Peru, to watch the ceremony—though there was some confusion among fans about whether they were witnessing the fictional wedding between the characters María and Don Esteban or a real wedding between the two actors who played the parts.

For our own festivity, Llorlli, the perky secretary, has brought a portable radio, which is blasting loud *salsa.* And Mercedes has brought a bottle of rum with which to christen the boat—the traditional breaking of the bottle on the bow. It doesn't take long before wiser heads prevail and we drink the rum instead. Bruno looks happy, deliriously so. He's surrounded by office girls in miniskirts and microminis.

It is indeed a glorious day. Clear blue skies. Frigate birds soaring overhead. A light but refreshing sea breeze. Fredo tries to back the boat and trailer onto the ramp, but he's not having much luck. It takes a knack, since the steering is counterintuitive. You have to turn the wheel to the left to back the trailer to the right and vice versa. The maneuver takes patience and finesse, and Fredo possesses neither.

He backs the trailer this way and that until it's sideways to the ramp. It looks as if he intends to launch the boat by tipping it over on its side. Frustrated, Fredo curses up a storm. Gods, saints, mothers, virgins, all receive his wrath. Bruno, who's more experienced at this, offers to take the wheel, but Fredo waves him off. He knows Bruno only wants to impress the women. He knows because that is precisely what he himself is trying to do. Instead, he must endure their playful taunts, their double entendres.

"*Qué pasa, Fredo?* You can't find the slot? Don't know how to put it in?" They start to chant: "*Métleo, Fredo!* Put it in! Put it in!"

At last—to loud cheers—Fredo manages to align the boat and trailer on the ramp. The moment has arrived. It's time for the launching of the R/V *Maroho*. I climb aboard. Almost immediately, I have to fend off boarders who want a ride in the boat. I tell them that after we launch I'll be happy to give them a little tour of the bay. But it will have to be a very short tour since the engine has to undergo its break-in period. Less than half speed for at least ten hours.

Mercedes is quite looped now. Her beehive hairdo has a starboard list as she staggers down to the boat for the traditional launching ceremony. After a few unintelligible benedictions, she whacks the bow with an empty bottle of rum. Chips of fiberglass fly everywhere, but the bottle remains unbroken. Another *whack!* More pieces of boat are chipped away. I beg her to stop, and thankfully she does so before she's put a hole in the bow.

Fredo and Bruno remove the tie-down straps from the boat. Then Fredo unclips the towline clamp from the bow ring, and the boat eases off the trailer and into the murky water. I lower the outboard drive unit, then turn on the exhaust blower for a full minute to prevent an explosion. I turn the ignition key on but can't seem to locate the starter toggle. Ah, there, located for whatever reason on the opposite side of the helm. I press the toggle and lo, the engine turns over. Smoke billows out of the exhaust vent on the stern with a loud sound of flatulence. I ease the throttle into reverse. And back ever so slowly into the bay. It's good to be standing on a bridge again, to feel the easy movement of sea and swell.

Back on the ramp they're still waving to me. Bruno and Fredo and Cruz-Cruz seem especially enthused. But no. There's an urgency to their gestures. They're waving me back in. Bruno is holding up something in his hand and pointing to it. I can't make out what it is. But his cries of "*Tapón! Tapón!*" carry over the water.

Then suddenly the engine quits. I press the starter toggle again. Nothing. Except the sound of soft gurgling. Water is bubbling up from somewhere aft and now it's sloshing across the deck. Already we're three feet down by the stern.

The R/V *Maroho,* the pride of the Puerto Rican Navy, is sinking.

CHAPTER 8
Whirling World

*A boat simply does not allow for genuine rest. Its essential na-
ture is peril, held in check only through enormous effort and
expense.*

—David Vann, *A Mile Down*

"Let us walk," says Gabriel Amador. We are in the tangled
gardens of Morcelo, a spiritual center set on a lush promontory overlooking San Juan and the sea beyond. Simple wood
cabins surround an airy, open meditation hall where New Age
disciples practice group yoga. The center's guiding light is the
Indian guru Jiddu Krishnamurti, who visited here recently.
Krishnamurti is given to Socratic dialogues with an Eastern
philosophical bent.

"Why do birds fly away when I come near?" a disciple
asked him.

"We kill the birds, torture them, catch them in nets, and put them in cages," he replied. Next question.

Gabriel, his wife Saskia, and their three little boys come up here almost every weekend. Saskia is a strikingly beautiful woman with an open and inquiring mind. She believes in UFOs, fairies, and auras. She's also convinced that Christ has returned to earth and is wandering around somewhere in Puerto Rico. The signs are everywhere: St. Elmo's fire on mountaintop antennae, luminescent jellies in the bays, and tree frogs that chant, Jeee-sus! Jeee-sus! Any day now He will make His presence known. Until then, we have Krishnamurti, the Buddha incarnate, for spiritual guidance.

Morcelo offers a respite from the maddening hubbub of San Juan. It's a serene haven, far from the whirling world, a place where healing energies converge and the mind can be flushed clean of negative thoughts. It's an especially good place to come to after watching one's future sink below the turbid waters of San Juan Bay.

As we stroll among the tree ferns and tulip trees and mountain orchids, Gabo offers an insightful quote from Kirshnamurti: "However big a problem may be. . . . only a mind that is unoccupied and therefore fresh can tackle and resolve the problem." Still, when it comes to the scuttling of the *Maroho*, it's the words of Jack London that come to mind instead: "The deep water sailor. . . . knows nothing. . . . Put him in a small boat and he is helpless. He will cut an even better figure on the hurricane deck of a horse."

The cause of the mishap was a small one; in fact, it weighs no more than a couple of ounces. "*Tapón! Tapón!*" Bruno had shouted. Boat plug. Damn! I forgot to check the boat plug! In fact, I never gave it a thought.

With the inrush of water, the boat began sinking by the stern. The engine was flooded and it quickly stalled. I hurried aft and I took off the engine cover. Seawater was bubbling up from somewhere in the engine well. I groped around in the oily water for the source of the leak. Countless gallons continued to pour in, but at last I found the drainage hole. I tore off my T-shirt and plugged the hole with it.

Soaking wet and streaked with engine grease, I grabbed a mooring line and raced up to the bow. Fredo and Bruno had already waded down the boat ramp to help, and I tossed them the line. Bruno caught it, and everyone ashore cheered "*Eso es!*" That's it! Then the wind kicked up and began pushing the boat away from them. Fredo and Bruno were in water up to their necks when they let go of the line. "*Ay noooo!*" from the crowd. This had become a spectator sport.

My heart was racing. The boat was drifting toward a busy ship channel. I tied together two mooring lines, coiled one end and tossed the coil toward Fredo and Bruno. "*Eso es!*" But the line fell just short of their reach. "*Ay noooo!*"

Fredo swam to the line and grabbed hold of it. Then, holding the bitter end in his teeth like a retriever with a stick, he dog-paddled toward the small pier adjacent to the ramp. But as the boat continued drifting out into the channel, the slack was quickly taken up. And there was Fredo, faithful Fredo, being towed out to sea by the line in his teeth. I quickly tied another line to the one he was holding and paid out enough for Fredo to reach the pier.

He passed the line up to Cruz-Cruz, and everyone took a hold of it—Gabo, Ambrosio, Mercedes, Bruno and the gaggle of office women—and together they hauled and hauled and hauled: "*Uno dos tres! Uno dos tres! Uno dos tres!*"

Cruz-Cruz barked orders like the artillery officer he once was, his platoon hauling four tons of boat, engine, and seawater against the wind while I bailed and bailed and bailed (they say the most effective instrument for bailing is a bucket in the hands of a frightened man) until slowly, ever so slowly, the boat came alongside the pier. "*Eso es!*"

Later, the launching festivities over, the crowd gone back to the office, Cruz-Cruz and I surveyed the damage. The engine was thoroughly flooded, and with salt water no less, the bane of all things metal. Cruz-Cruz simply shook his head and said "*Ay, bendito,*" the quintessential Puerto Rican expression of fatigue, empathy, pity, and resignation.

I suppose I could put the blame for the fiasco on the boat's design—the odd location of the drainage hole making it easy to overlook—or even on Llorlli's panties, the sight of which distracted Bruno from handing me the boat plug in the first place. But any savvy boat skipper would have checked for a boat plug before launching.

"Ah, but you will learn from this," says Gabo, putting a consoling hand on my shoulder as we walk the gardens of Morcelo. But I doubt it. As an old seaman once told me, "A captain is a man who knows a great deal about very little, and as he goes along he knows more and more about less and less, until he finally knows practically everything about nothing."

I do know this: the engine will have to be thoroughly flushed, its components disassembled and carefully cleaned. And I know this too: It will not be done yesterday. Making it very unlikely that the boat will be ready for the scheduled start of whatever the governor is contemplating for Culebra.

And Culebra is everywhere in the news now. A contingent of Culebrans has arrived in Washington, DC, to present their case to Congress—in particular to the House Armed Services Committee, whose chairman is Representative Lucius Mendel Rivers, a war hawk and white supremacist from Gumville, South Carolina. Rivers is renowned for his plan to bring peace in Vietnam: "I say get 'em by the balls, and their hearts and minds will follow."

But first, the islanders will appeal to the Real Estate Subcommittee, chaired by Representative Charles Edward Bennett of Jacksonville, Florida, another war hawk and segregationist. It is this subcommittee that must first approve the Navy's new plan for Culebra.

In the wake of the initial uproar over the proposal to evict all the residents of Culebra, the Navy has had a change of heart.

"The Navy did not fully realize the feelings of the people of Culebra," announced Rear Admiral Alfred R. Matter, commander of the Caribbean Sea Frontier. There will be no mass evictions. Further, "to smooth troubled waters," the Navy will ask Congress to release an additional 680 acres to the Culebrans, including ten miles of shoreline. Still, an additional 2,200 acres will be expropriated from Culebra proper to create "safety zones."

"The Navy's plan is nothing but a trick," said an angry Mayor Feliciano. "The Navy gives us 680 acres that we now use and takes away 2,200 acres that we had planned for development."

On the first day of hearings, more than a hundred Puerto Ricans, mostly from Culebra, have crowded into the committee room. It will be an uphill fight. "We know ahead of time," says one Culebran, "that the committee is of the Navy, by the Navy, and for the Navy."

Historically, Puerto Ricans have not had much luck in their dealings with Washington. At the turn of the nineteenth century, the new American administrators didn't quite know what to make of their subjects. They often mistook graciousness for indolence, courtesy for complacency. A new word for its citizens was coined: "spiggotys." It was a "synonym for the Porto Rico native" who often greeted the Americans with the phrase "I speak a de English." "Speak a de" became "spiggoty" which was later shortened to "spic."

Another casualty of the Spanish-American War was Puerto Rico's name. It became *Porto Rico.* Some historians say the name of the island was misspelled in the Treaty of Paris wherein Spain ceded the island to the United States. Others claim the spelling was instituted to make it easier for the island's new administrators to pronounce its name.

Whatever the reason, the new possession was thereafter called Porto Rico. From the outset, Puerto Ricans protested. But soon the name Porto Rico appeared on US navigation charts and in congressional documents, newspaper articles, and school textbooks. Puerto Rican writers, scholars, and histori-

ans made entreaties to Washington requesting that the rightful
name be restored. The response from Congress was predictable.
Why go through the inconvenience and expense of changing
the spelling just to appease these . . . these . . . Who are these
people anyway?

Then in 1912 a group of Puerto Rican leaders arranged
a meeting with President William Howard Taft. His Corpu-
lence, as Taft was known, invited them to dinner. The story
is recounted in Wagenheim's *The Puerto Ricans*: "The meal was
splendid," the Mayor of San Juan later reported, "and after-
wards the President invited us into his office to discuss affairs."
They were presenting their case for the restoration of the island's name "when suddenly we heard a loud snore," wrote the
mayor, "and everyone fell silent. President Taft, a man with an
enormous abdomen, had dozed off."

"*Ajo!*" whispered Don Mateo Fajardo. "The rascal has fallen
asleep on us."

To the Americans, it was the Puerto Ricans who were slum-
bering and had been doing so for four hundred years.

In *The Islands: The Worlds of the Puerto Ricans*, Stan Steiner
quotes the first American governor: "These children of the sun
have learned to rely too much on the kindness of Nature." They
would surely benefit from the "indomitable thrift and industry
which has always marked the pathway of the Anglo-Saxon."

"They are not fighters as the Cubans," expounded a Senator
Henry M. Teller from Colorado. "Such a race does not deserve
citizenship." That seemed to be the consensus.

Nor did Puerto Ricans deserve the right to vote.

"Why put votes in the hands of men who can make no intelligent use of them?" opined the *New York Times*. As if Betances, de Hostos, Baldorioty, de Diego, Muñoz Rivera, Celso Barbosa—all brilliant, multi-faceted, multi-lingual political leaders—never existed.

For the next half-century the island was ruled by a series of governors appointed by the US president. None spoke Spanish.

Rep. Bennett opens the proceedings by questioning the Culebrans' motives. It's his understanding, he says, that land speculators are behind the protests. There's an audible *no, no, no* from the Culebrans.

The mayor then informs the congressman that, yes, Culebrans want to be free to develop their own properties for tourism, farming, and cattle raising, but on the lands now claimed by the Navy they would set up nature preserves, marine parks, recreation areas, and a historical center. He reminds the committee that Culebra and Vieques are the only inhabited islands in the entire world that are used for target practice. And he says that Culebrans have suffered and sacrificed enough for the national defense. "We have nothing against the Americans. We have nothing against the Navy. We only want to be left in peace."

Some twenty witnesses appear before the subcommittee. The first witnesses testify to the relentlessness of the shelling. Every year more than six thousand aircraft make between thirty-five thousand and forty thousand target runs. Explosions shake the island nine and a half hours a day, except on Sundays when it is three and a half hours.

Other witnesses speak of the mental and emotional anguish islanders experience, living under a continual state of siege. A mother describes the deafening roar of jets that awaken her children at all hours of the night: "Children can't sleep in Culebra when the Navy is firing."

Perhaps the most poignant testimony comes from the mayor's brother Carmelo, a school teacher.

"Teaching in Culebra is an extremely difficult job," he says, with "the continuous flow of air traffic at low altitudes over the school, helicopters, jets, prop planes making an infernal noise, creating a state of tension and anxiety and rendering it impossible to hold the attention of the students. When the bombs and shells are exploding, the school buildings tremble with every explosion. You can see the fear in the children's eyes."

But Subcommittee Chairman Bennett appears unmoved. In a tone that's both condescending and chastising, he says that the sacrifices Culebrans have made are no worse than those made by the people of his own district, where the Department of Defense owns a considerable amount of land.

"And how often do they bomb this land?" asks Mayor Feliciano. Bennett ignores the question and moves to adjourn the day's session. But he assures the witnesses that his subcommittee will consider the Culebrans concerns "very carefully."

"*Ñoña!*" says Adaír. Bullshit.
"*Exacto!*" says Blanquita.

Like most in Puerto Rico, the *amigos* at Pepe's Place have been faithfully following the story on the local television news. The Culebrans, we agree, appear to have acquitted themselves quite well. They voiced their concerns with a simple and honest eloquence. But will it be enough?

"The Navy is like a ghost," says Carmelo Feliciano. "It is everywhere. In the water, in the air, on the land, and in the earth. But we cannot speak with it."

The following day it's the Navy's turn to present its case. Rear Admiral Norwell G. Ward offers a belated apology for the ill-timed shelling of Flamenco Beach, calling it a "Navy mistake," and assures the committee that such mistakes are in the past. Then he stresses the highly desirable location of the island for gunnery exercises, and the $300 million already invested in the Atlantic Fleet Weapons Range. Still, as a gesture of good will, the Navy will make available surplus egg incubators to the Culebrans.

A procession of uniforms and suits follows the Admiral.

"As far as the military is concerned," says a uniform, "it is impossible for the Navy to give up its use of the island of Culebra for target practice. It's a vital part of the Atlantic Fleet Weapons Range."

"The Navy has conducted several studies to determine if there is a satisfactory alternative to the Puerto Rican training area," offers another. "The answer is no."

A congressman asks about using floating targets instead. "Such targets couldn't withstand intense naval gunfire," says a defense industry spokesman, "nor could such a floating platform survive even a single strike from a Walleye missile." The

Walleye is a powerful "smart bomb," the first of its generation, a precision-guided missile with an 850 lb. high-explosive warhead. It's maneuvered to its target with the aid of a television camera in its nose. Perhaps the most malevolent use of the boob tube yet.

I remember standing watch aboard a ship at Fort Stockton on the Sacramento River as Walleyes were being loaded. About a dozen feet long, they're sleek, finned missiles with a glass "eye" on the tip of the nose like the eye of a giant squid. "Fat Albert" is what they call the Walleye in Vietnam, from the lovable character in Bill Cosby's stand-up routine. It's a rather endearing nickname for something designed to destroy whole villages with a single strike.

And it is these monster missiles that will be tested on the island of Culebra. The "footprint" of these weapons—that is, the zone of destruction—is huge. There is no margin for error, hence the need for an additional 2,200 acres on Culebra itself as a safety zone.

"It's for the Culebrans' own safety and welfare that the real estate transfer must be approved," says another witness for the Navy.

We have to destroy the village, in order to save it.

As he adjourns the hearings, Rep. Bennett reminds the witnesses that a decision on the Navy plan will not come soon. There's still much to investigate, to deliberate, to ruminate. He even suggests that some sort of compromise might be found between the Navy and the Culebrans.

In Pepe's Place, there is guarded optimism regarding Culebra's chances of seeing a halt to the bombing. "The peoples of
Culebra have spoken . . . *con dignidad*," says Wilfredo with the
dog named Puppy, "*y con elocuencia.*"

"At the very least," says Pepe, "they have been shown a to-
ken of respect."

"It's Puerto Rican Power!" says Ramón.

"*Exacto!*" says Blanquita.

Yes, the Culebrans acquitted themselves well on the national stage. But there were other constituents whose interests
went undefended that day. Snappers and sea turtles and zenaida doves. They and all the denizens of the mangroves, seagrass
beds, and coral reefs also are suffering. For these, the bombing is lethal. But among politicians and press alike, it's hard to
generate sympathy for the plight of a piping plover or spotted
goatfish. Sure, a few charismatic species attract attention sometimes. But the powers-that-be are just not that empathic toward the nonhuman creatures with which we share the planet.

CHAPTER 9
Spit in the Ocean

Every hawk has its pestering finch.
—Puerto Rican proverb

In the *San Juan Star*, a short article appears on page eight under the banner, TEAM TO UNDERTAKE CULEBRA STUDY. The Department of Public Works, it states, will assemble a team of specialists in mineral, soil, and water resources; fauna, flora, and ecosystems; fish and sea floor resources. The team will explore Culebra to assess the impact of naval operations on the environment and prepare a full report for the Environmental Quality Board of Puerto Rico.

This brief, prosaic announcement signals something more: Governor Luis A. Ferré is taking action at last.

I come into the office one day to find a barely legible message taped up on the drywall. It's from Cruz-Cruz, about an urgent meeting that I must attend. I'm already late for it. I slip

87

quietly into the office of Dr. Cruz A. Matos, newly appointed head of the Environmental Quality Board. Other members of the Culebra research team are already there, sipping coffee and munching on *buñuelos de nubes*, "cloud muffins," and discussing the upcoming venture.

Most of the team members are familiar faces from the Area of Natural Resources. But there are also professors from the University of Puerto Rico and scientists from federal agencies such as the US Geological Survey and the US Fish and Wildlife Service. They have all been recruited by Matos, a black Puerto Rican from New York and a brilliant and articulate Oxford graduate. Matos gazes on the world with hooded eyes. He's a man who is often underestimated.

The team leader is Robert Cassagnol, a tall Haitian who's an expert in coastal geology. Cassagnol brings up the scheduling challenges the team faces. The governor, he says, needs the full report submitted ASAP. That means the team has a little over a month to prep, conduct the field studies, and write the report. The team members exchange dubious looks.

"It takes us a month just to gather the equipment," says a geologist from the USGS.

"*Coño,* it takes us a month to order a pencil," says Ambrosio. Others grumble, "What's the rush?" and "We need to do these studies right" The consensus is that four weeks isn't enough time.

"It will have to be," says Matos, "because Governor Ferré has a scheduled meeting with the president. He wants to deliver the report directly to him."

"Nixon?"

"Yes. The governor hopes to convince the president that Culebra should be protected on environmental grounds. But he needs supportive evidence."

The newly signed National Environmental Policy Act of 1969 is a political work of art, stunningly beautiful for its conciseness, its minimalism, its resonance. NEPA requires that every proposal for federal action that will have a significant impact on the environment must include an Environmental Impact Statement (EIS), which is to be submitted to a Council on Environmental Quality (CEQ) for approval. Thus government agencies are compelled, for the first time, to take environmental quality into account in their decision-making process. After only a year the EIS has already proved revolutionary. Stateside citizens groups have used it to halt the building of nuclear power plants, twelve-lane freeways, and oil rigs on the continental shelf.

The Navy has insisted that it is exempt from these environmental regulations. It argues that national security trumps environmental concerns. This contention has been challenged by Culebra's dedicated young lawyers, Richard Copaken and Tom Jones. Based in Washington, DC, with the law firm Covington and Burling, the two have been working *pro bono* on the Culebra issue for almost a year now. Copaken, in particular, has proved to be persistent and determined. He brought the Navy's assertions to the committee that wrote the bill. The committee promptly informed the Navy brass that the Navy is not above the nation's environmental laws. It will have to file an Environmental Impact Statement.

But can an EIS truly stop the bombing of Culebra? First, the Navy itself will be filing the statement and thus conducting the research. One can only imagine how impartial that report will be. Even an unbiased study might have difficulty proving that Culebra is worth protecting at all. The island is arid and mostly treeless, with sparse grasslands and no minerals. Its only natural resources appear to be abundant mosquitoes, countless lizards, and pervasive thorn bushes. In the words of one naval officer, Culebra is a spit in the ocean.

Perhaps Ferré is hoping that the team will uncover some hidden resources that can be used to contradict the Navy's assertion that the island is useful only as a bombing range. Though no one on the team is privy to the governor's motives, there is a collective shift in attitude on learning that he will deliver the report directly to the president. If nothing else, the move will demonstrate to Nixon that Puerto Ricans intend to use every legal means available to save Culebra. And who knows, the team may discover some environmental treasures after all.

Cruz-Cruz will coordinate the efforts of the marine scientists. But right from the outset he must deal with one significant underachiever: The R/V *Maroho*.

"And the boat?" he asks *sotto voce*.

The boat is slated to be used in the survey of Culebra's marine environment: the mangroves and turtle grass beds and coral reefs. And the R/V *Maroho*—soaked to the ribs, engine dead, battery dead, bilge pump dead, gauges out of whack—is not quite ready to go.

I shrug my shoulders.

"It is now yesterday!" whispers Cruz-Cruz.

One of the team comes up to us; he's the only one besides me in work shirt, khakis, and boat shoes.

"*Capitán*," says Cruz-Cruz. "Meet Francisco Torrejón. He's our marine biologist. You two will be working together."

Mucho gusto and a firm handshake. That handshake will mark the beginning of a lifelong friendship. Francisco is in his twenties, just a few years older than me. He's a small man, strikingly handsome, with expressive eyes. He exudes energy.

"So, *Capitán*. How is your boat?" he asks, with a grin that suggests he knows *exactly* how the damn boat is.

"We've had some problems. Still working out the bugs. But nothing major," I say, trying to project the same can-do spirit as the rest of the team.

"Why don't you join me tomorrow?" he asks. "I will be diving off Caja de Muertos. It is a small island just off Ponce. It would be good for you to see the kind of work we will be doing in Culebra. And you will see some beautiful reefs."

"I'd like to. But I think I'm going to be busy with the boat. You know, routine maintenance and all that."

"Well, if you can find some free time it would be very worthwhile. I will be diving there all this week."

"Actually, I've never been scuba diving."

"If you can breathe and you can swim, you can scuba. It is like learning how to juggle. All you need is the balls. Ha-haha!"

CHAPTER 10
Gardens of Stone

We still think of the sea as another world populated by weird or fierce animals, when in fact there is a striking unity of life above and under the surface of the oceans.
——Jacques Yves Cousteau

It's early dawn when Francisco swings by my house with a thirteen-foot Boston Whaler in tow. Even before my coffee has had a chance to kick in, I'm treated to the first pun of the day.

"So, *Capitán* . . . What do they call it when killer whales sing?"

"Isn't it a bit early for this?"

"An <u>orca</u>-stra. Hahahaaa!"

Francisco loves nothing more than a bad pun in English. And I'm to be subjected to many of them on the long drive to Ponce. There's little traffic as we drive over the mountains of the

Cordillera Central toward the south coast. En route, he tells me about his studies. He's a graduate student at the University of Florida, but he's come back home to Puerto Rico to work on his doctoral thesis. It's on something called coral reef succession. Succession is the natural pattern of ecosystem change as a reef slowly expands and builds over the centuries.

The rising sun has already warmed the dark sands of La Guancha, a seaside village near Playa de Ponce, as we back the trailer down the boat ramp. The Ponce Yacht Club is on one side of the bay, the public dock on the other. While Francisco parks the rig, I maneuver the Whaler alongside the dock.

A boy sees the scuba tanks in the boat and yells, "Jock Couteau!" My chest swells.

With Francisco at the helm, we zip along with the boat up on a plane (a thrill denied me on the *Maroho*) toward Caja de Muertos, an arid island about five miles from La Guancha. The sea is sleeping late this morning and is barely stirring. But the flying fish are awake, and they skip merrily across the waters like scaled stones.

On the western end of the mile-long island is Cerro Morillo. Steep, bare, and craggy, the hill is shaped like a witch's hat. On the island's eastern end is a taller hill, dotted with cactus and topped by a weathered, gray lighthouse. Like the island itself, the lighthouse is deserted.

We head to the southeast corner of the island, which faces the open Caribbean. It can get rough here, but it's where the most extensive reefs lie. As we motor toward the line of fringing reef, I can see amorphous brown and green shapes just below the surface. Mounds of star or brain coral, perhaps. The water is remarkably clear and appears much shallower than it actually is. Only experience can teach the subtle shadings of color that indicate the water's depth. When the water is calm like this, it creates an optical illusion that the ocean bottom is rising up as you move over it—and that you are about to run aground, a particular anxiety of mine.

I have a recurring dream in which I'm alone on the bridge of a merchant ship, and I make a simple arithmetic error on a lighthouse bearing that puts us on a wrong heading. The result is a deafening *crunch*—the ship lurches to a halt—sirens, whistles, shouts. The ship heels over—the captain's face is in mine as he shouts, *Idiot! We're aground!* Next thing I know, I'm bobbing in a life raft with surly seamen who curse me under their breaths: *Idiot! He ran us aground!*

Francisco cuts the engine, and we slowly glide ahead, passing over a large patch of elkhorn coral. He turns the boat seaward into a wisp of breeze, and the boat slows and stops.

"You can't just drop the anchor anywhere," he says. "You could damage the corals. I like to hand carry the anchor down to the bottom and set it in a big patch of sand."

Before I can say "Makes sense to me," Francisco, anchor in hand, is over the side. No grass grows under this man's feet.

Moments later, he surfaces. "We're in about fifteen feet of water. Pay out about a hundred feet. That should hold us. I'll make sure the anchor's set." Before I can say "Sure thing," he's gone again. He stays down below until I've paid out the line and he's checked that the anchor is holding. The man must have the lungs of a whale.

Back on board, it's time for Scuba 101. Francisco teaches the whole course in about three minutes. First he strips off the little rubber strap that holds my snorkel to my mask, and runs the snorkel through the mask strap instead.

"Keep everything simple," he says. He himself has no buoyancy compensation vest, no wetsuit, not even a dive watch. "We won't be going below twenty feet today, so we don't need all that stuff."

"OK. Under twenty feet. No need for stuff."

"You must remember two things: first, keep breathing slow and steady, and second, when you come back up, don't rise faster than your bubbles."

"Breathe slow and steady. Don't rise faster than bubbles."

"*Bueno.* Now, if your ears hurt, pinch your nose and blow until the pain subsides."

"Ears hurt. Pinch nose. Blow."

"*Exacto.* One other thing: if your mask gets too much water in it, just press a finger to the top of the mask like this, tilt your head back, and blow through your nose."

"Press mask, tilt head back, blow through nose."

"*Bueno. Perfecto. Excelente.* You pass the course."

"That's it?"

"*Eso es.*"

"But what about, you know, dive tables and decompression sickness and nitrogen narcosis and rhapsody of the deep and . . . and . . ."

He straps on my weight belt and tank, sticks the regulator into my mouth, and with an "*Adiós!*" shoves me over the side.

I sink like a stone.

Breathe, breathe, breathe! Jesus, my ears are killing me! Pinch and blow. Pinch and blow. Oh, cripes, I'm on the bottom already! Sitting on the frigging bottom. How'd I get down here so fast? Breathe, breathe, breathe!

Moments later there's an explosion of bubbles overhead, and Francisco slowly descends until he's standing next me in the sands. I'm still sitting on the bottom like a pile of used car parts. He gives me the OK sign with a questioning look. I signal back: OK. Except for the water in my mask. *Press glass, tilt back, blow! There. Clear as a nun's conscience.*

OK? signals Francisco again. OK, I signal. Follow me, he indicates with a wave. And we're off. *Breathe, breathe, breathe!*

Soon the splendor of the silent world overcomes all feelings of trepidation. We approach a thick cluster of staghorn corals surrounded by fluorescent yellow tube sponges. Purple sea fan corals wave in the gentle current like sirens in a water ballet. Francisco indicates we should remain where we are, simply hovering and observing. In no time, countless fishes emerge from their hiding places to resume the dramas of their daily lives. Little blue chromis dart out from the coral branches and rise up toward the surface to feed on plankton. They pick off the invisible creatures one by one. The chromis in turn are chased by a posse of yellowtail snappers who pick *them* off one by one.

Now I'm surrounded by a swirl of glittering blue, a huge school of blue tangs. It's like being in the center of a cyclone. I turn with them as they swirl around me. As suddenly as they appeared, the blue tangs are gone and I'm spinning alone.

A big, fat-lipped grouper comes up to me, pauses about a foot in front of my mask, and gives me a look that seems to ask if I really belong here. He lumbers over to Francisco, who reaches out and tickles his chin.

Then I see something out of the corner of my eye. It's a great barracuda—no, there are two of them—no, a whole wolf pack of barracuda—working their jaws as if preparing for an attack. My heart is suddenly racing. *Breath, breathe, breathe!* I point them out to Francisco. He gives me the OK sign. No worries.

Then he points out a pair of butterfly fish probing the reef for coral polyps. *Yes, Francisco,* I want to say, *the butterfly fish are interesting. But what about these six-foot predators gaping hungrily at us? Should we not pay them some mind?*

Apparently not. When I point to them again, he waves me off and turns his attention to a little damselfish. He appears irate at Francisco for intruding on his territory. Francisco wiggles his fingers at the fish, and the feisty fellow pecks at them fiercely.

It's then I see something large swimming directly toward me. It's a giant eagle ray about seven feet wide, wing tip to wing tip, with a long, whiplike tail. And the chase is on. No, not the ray pursuing me. But Francisco pursuing the ray. The man is utterly fearless, or crazy. I can't decide which. The ray finally eludes his grasp and veers off, flashing its white underbelly. Then it disappears into the indigo deep.

We beach the Whaler on the white sand of a quiet cove, then walk up a gentle rise overlooking the turtle grass flats and sit down to lunch. Francisco passes me a Cubano sandwich thick with roast pork, ham, cheese, and pickles.

"You did good," he says. "You didn't drown."

"I had a very thorough instructor."

"We should do a night dive some time. That's when the reef really comes to life." Corals may look like plants, he says, but they are actually colonies of little animals. "Each tiny polyp looks like a flower vase, its rim ringed with tentacles. They use their tentacles to capture plankton. And they do this at night."

Living inside the polyps are countless single-celled algae, Francisco explains. The algae convert carbon dioxide into oxygen, which the polyps "breathe." The algae also produce sugars, a kind of energy bar that the corals need to extract calcium from the seawater. It is this calcium that the coral animals use to create a limestone exoskeleton.

"It takes millions of layers of exoskeleton and thousands of years to create the reef," he says. "Which is about as long as it takes to get paid by the Puerto Rican government." He knows about that, too.

As corals replicate themselves, they take on shapes—of branches, antlers, leaves, shrubs, or domes, depending on the species. The reefs they create provide habitat and sustenance for seaweeds and fungi, sponges and echinoderms, crabs and lobsters, reptiles and marine mammals, and countless colorful species of fish.

"It is the richest ecosystem on earth," Francisco says. "Except, perhaps, for the Amazon. I hope to go to the Amazon some day. But until I do, the reefs of Puerto Rico will do me just fine."

He tells me what he looks for when assessing the health of a reef, the things we'll need to make note of in Culebra. Is the water clean and clear? Is there a good variety of soft and hard corals? Are the corals healthy? Do they show signs of bleaching? Bleaching is when the corals turn white because the algae have died; this can be caused by rising temperatures or sedimentation or pollution or even overfishing. He looks for signs of disease, such as white band or black band disease, which can decimate an entire reef. He takes note of breakage from storms, nets, anchors, or pilferage.

"You know those roadside stands selling dead coral?" he says. "Never buy from them. They are destroying the reefs."

Too late. I have a bleached white branch of staghorn coral sitting on my desk at home.

"You also want to see plenty of top predators like jacks and groupers. Snappers. Barracudas. They feed on the algae grazers, the parrotfish and damselfish and blue tangs."

"I was in a cloud of blue tangs."

"You have to be careful with them. They have bright yellow blades near their dorsal fins that are razor sharp. The blue tangs are like pirates. There are these tiny, little fish that actually raise algae, like farmers. And the blue tangs will attack them, slashing at them with their blades. They will chase the farmer fish away and devour their algae. So if you fish out the groupers and snappers, you get too many blue tangs. Too many tangs chase off the farmer fish. No farmer fish and the algae disappears.

Without algae, the coral bleaches and dies. Everything in the reef must be in perfect balance."

I'm beginning to see why this unimposing young graduate student was recruited for the Culebra study. Francisco is a passionate conservationist with an encyclopedic knowledge of Puerto Rico's marine life.

We decide to take a post-prandial hike up to the lighthouse of Caja de Muertos. We follow a rough path littered with pocked stones. The brush is thick, thorny, and thoroughly inhospitable. Lizards scurry about. The acrid smell of dried bird shit is in the air. The island was once named Utía for the countless little nutria-like rodents that scampered about. The locals boiled them up with nuts and honey.

"They're almost extinct now," says Francisco. "In all the times I've been here, I think I might have seen five or six."

Sometime in the nineteenth century, the island was given its present name, Caja de Muertos, or Coffin Island. Francisco tells me the story behind the island's name.

Back in the early eighteen hundreds, the island was a hideout for a pirate called José the Portuguese. Once, when he was trading his spoils in a market in St. Thomas, he saw a beautiful young woman. When he asked about her, he learned she was married. Still, José pursued her in the courtly manner of the times, with flowers, love poems, and trinkets of gold. Then her husband died suddenly, and she consented to marry José. But the pirate's happiness was short-lived, for she too died in a plague that swept the islands. Heartbroken, he had her embalmed by the finest practitioner of the art in all the Caribbean. He then placed her in a coffin like no other. The base was sheathed in copper and the lid was solid glass. He brought the coffin to the island and hid it in a cave. He would return to this hiding place after every raid and lovingly gaze upon her corpse through the coffin window.

Despite all the gold and silver he plundered, José the Portuguese was forever in mourning. The fight had gone out of him. Finally, he was caught and hanged. His fellow pirates searched the island for buried treasure, but all they found was the coffin. They took the woman's body out of the coffin and ransomed her remains to her relatives in St. Thomas.

"So what happened to the coffin?" I ask.

"Believe it or not, they found it recently. In a cave on Cerro Morillo. That big hill over there. And the copper sheathing and the glass top were still in perfect condition."

By the time we reach the lighthouse, we're sweating buckets and winded from the hike. I gaze up at the tower's cracked and crumbling edifice and don't relish climbing the rusting metal stairs that wind up to the tower.

"*Vámonos!*" says Francisco, like a kid coming upon monkey bars.

Clank, clank, clank. Up the century-old steps we climb. Many are rusted through in places. Finally we reach the tower. The view through the open windows is spectacular. To the north: the harbor of Ponce, the white city; to the east: the gleaming salt flats of Salinas; to the west: the myriad cays of Guayanilla; and to the south: the Caribbean, a sea of diamonds glittering in the afternoon sun.

Francisco says that from here we can observe the forces that cause a coral reef to develop—or not. It all depends on the relationships between the sea, the shelf, and the prevailing winds. On the north shore facing Ponce, the bottom is uniformly shallow and sheltered from the wind. There are quiet coves lined with mangroves, and salt flats dotted with turtle grass beds. There are a few patch reefs, but nothing as impressive as the reefs on the opposite shore facing the open Caribbean, where we were diving. There the shelf deepens, and the water, scoured by currents, is clear. The fringing reef is long and wide.

I ask him if the reefs off Culebra are as healthy as this one.

"The Navy controls all the beaches, and limits where you can take a boat. So no one has been able to study the reefs. The local fishermen say they are incredible. At least in the areas that have not been shelled. As for the reefs in the firing range, we've heard stories about one-ton bombs blasting huge holes in them. The Navy denies using bombs that big. But who knows?"

"I guess they'd never let us dive the reefs in the firing range."

"No, they would not."

"Then what's the point of our going there?"

After a long moment, he simply says, "We shall see."

Later, we don masks and fins and wade into the white sand shallows on the northern shore. As we snorkel across the flats, the dappled light on the sandy bottom is almost psychedelic. Francisco warns me away from long-spined sea urchins nestled among the conchs and turtle grass.

A peacock-colored flatfish comes gliding by like a flying carpet with fins. It dips down and buries itself in the sand. Then a lone boxfish hovers before my mask like a miniature submarine. Flutter, flutter and it's gone. A big queen triggerfish cruises the shallows for prey. With its gaudy makeup, it does look like a queen—a San Francisco queen. An even stranger-looking fish comes walking along the bottom. Suddenly it splays out its huge blue pectoral fins; they look like the scalloped fans of a flamenco dancer. The fish is a flying gurnard, whose "wings" will make it a difficult meal for the triggerfish to swallow.

Soon I'm surrounded by a silver cloud of tiny fish flashing in the sunlight. The fish move in unison, with lightning speed and astonishing coordination, like a drill corps. And they're gone.

"Did you see that huge school of silver fish?" I ask, as we toss our gear back into the boat.

"They are juvenile jacks," says Francisco. "The seagrass beds are the nursery grounds for the reefs. They also trap a lot of sediment and keep the waters around the reef clean and clear. In Culebra they say the seagrass beds are amazingly productive. There is even a lagoon that is so rich in dinoflagellates it is bioluminescent. It glows in the dark. I have always wanted to see it. And we will."

We ease the boat back into the water and head for the dock at Playa de Ponce. Over beers in an outdoor café, Francisco and I talk about our families. Like me, Francisco married young. He met his wife, Olga, when they were both undergraduates at the University of Puerto Rico. She's a good-hearted woman, but very shy. They have two little boys. The younger one, he says with pride, is a holy terror. Both learned to swim as infants.

We watch a little boat, loaded down to the rails with fishermen, putt-putt across the cove from the café. It turns down a waterway into the slums of Playa de Ponce. The boat disappears into a maze of shacks on stilts, all crowded together on fetid waters.

"The shacks remind me of the ones along *Barrio Cantera*," I say. "The ones along the Martín Peña Canal."

"I know Cantera well," Francisco says. He studies the flimsy hovels across the waters. "I was born in Cantera."

I'm pretty stunned by this.

His mother, he tells me, was a drug addict and a prostitute. A few months after he was born, she put him up for adoption with a Catholic agency. He was taken home by a dentist and his wife, from Humacao. "I was such a cute little bugger, they just couldn't resist." His new parents, he says, were all you could want in a mother and father.

"I guess you were pretty lucky."

"*Sí,* I was very lucky." His adoptive father loved boats, loved the ocean. He shared that passion with his son. "He wasn't a diver. Or much of a fisherman either. He just loved being out on the water."

We take our beers down to the dock, where local kids are pointing excitedly at something in the water. "*Tarpón!*" they shout.

Francisco shoos a seagull from its meal and picks up a few scraps of fish. The kids gather around him as he tosses the scraps into the murky waters. Suddenly a great silvery fish explodes out of the water and plunges back in with a big splash.

"*Ay, que monstro!*" shouts a boy of about ten or eleven. What a monster!

Francisco turns to me. "Did you see the size of that fish? My goodness!" he exclaims. "My goodness" is his most profane expression.

Francisco gives the boy the rest of the fish scraps, and the boy tosses a piece into the water. The great fish makes another spectacular appearance. The kids shriek with delight.

The boy, Carlito—barefoot, in a ragged T-shirt and shorts—tells us that the season is young and the big females have not yet arrived. His father once caught one that was almost 200 lb. with a shrimp no bigger than his pinky finger.

The fin of the tarpon cuts through the thick soup of the bay.

"The water's pretty polluted here," says Francisco. "If the tarpon can survive here, they can survive anywhere."

The same could be said of Francisco.

CHAPTER 11
Rio Loco

To the United States, bounded on the north by the Aurora Bo-
realis, on the south by the Precession of the Equinoxes, on the
east by Primeval Chaos, on the west by the Day of Judgment.
—A nineteenth-century toast.

The baby is somewhere in his room, crying. But who can
find him among the rubble of mooring lines, anchors,
boat cushions, personal flotation devices, charts, sextants, plot-
ting tools, binoculars, fire extinguishers, cookware, drogues,
marlinespikes, dive masks, snorkels, sheath knives, bosun whistles, nautical books, emergency flares, navigation lights, chains,
shackles, and rolls of biodegradable toilet paper? Cruz-Cruz's
monster compass sits atop the tallest pile, standing guard over
it all.

"Where is Brett?" cries Sonia.

"Don't worry," I say. "He's in there somewhere. Look. There. Under the canvas tarp. Right next to the case of WD-40." Sonia's patience is wearing thin, but I can't keep the stuff in the boatyard or in my door-less, wall-less office. We'd be cleaned out quicker than you could say "*Ay, Dios mío!*"

I go to the boatyard almost daily to check in on the *Maroho,* hoping to see signs of progress in the flushing and cleaning of its engine. But no, it sits on its trailer, swathed in a layer of fiberglass dust, ignored and unloved. I pester Bruno, the foreman, and all he says is, "*Capitán.* The engine is almost fixed." This seems a tad implausible, for no mechanic has been seen working on the engine since I brought the boat here long weeks ago. When I bring this to Bruno's attention he says, "Oh, the mechanic has been working. You just don't see him."

"But where is he now?"

"Is a holiday. Nobody working today."

"But there was no one working on it Friday either."

"*Sí, sí.* Holiday. That was a holiday too."

One of the joys of being a citizen by conquest is that one gets to celebrate one's own holidays as well those of the conqueror. There are nineteen official holidays on the calendar of the Commonwealth of Puerto Rico. Many were bestowed by the US federal government, but others are truly Puerto Rican, and the result is a wonderful redundancy. There's Christmas Day on December 25 and Three Kings Day on January 6. Fiestas and gift-giving and paid holidays occur on both days. There is Independence Day on July 4, as well as Constitution Day, commemorating when Puerto Rico became a US Commonwealth. There's Columbus Day, honoring his arrival in the New

World in 1492, and Discovery of Puerto Rico Day, honoring his arrival here in 1493.

Puerto Ricans celebrate Presidents' Day as well as four other holidays honoring Puerto Rican statesmen. Eugenio María de Hostos's Birthday, for the abolitionist lawyer and champion of independence. José de Diego's Birthday, for the statesman and poet whose poem about a doomed love affair was a two-hankie hit in the nineteenth century. Luis Muñoz Rivera's Birthday, for the architect of Puerto Rico's autonomy from Spain. And José Celso Barbosa's Birthday, for the founder of the first political party advocating US statehood.

Puerto Ricans also celebrate the unofficial US holidays like Mother's Day, Father's Day and Valentine's Day. Halloween has become popular, featuring *niños* in homemade costumes knocking on doors and chanting what to them is a nonsense rhyme: "Treek oh tree. Allo-ween. Treek oh tree. Allo-ween."

During Spanish colonial times there were more than forty religious feast days replete with masses, prayers, and processions as well as penitential bouts of drinking, feasting, and dancing. These holidays survive today in the festivals that honor the patron saint of a city, town, village, or street. While the religious aspects have faded, the partying has survived, with some *fiestas* lasting as long as a week.

But for the captain of the *Maroho,* there are no holidays. I have a lot of preparing to do and a lot to learn in the few weeks that remain before we set sail for the Spanish Virgins.

Francisco suggests that I visit the Marine Research Station, run by the University of Puerto Rico, to observe first-hand the kinds of research that are done from smaller vessels. He received his undergraduate degree through UPR's marine science program and he still has a number of contacts there.

The research station is located on Isla Magueyes, a small island just offshore of the fishing village of La Parguera in the southeast corner of Puerto Rico.

But he warns me, "When you go, it should be during the new moon."

La Parguera has an unusual claim to fame: it is home to what is called the Phosphorescent Bay. It glows in the dark. The phenomenon is even more impressive on a moonless night. The bay is one of only a half dozen or so in the world that are permanently bioluminescent. Puerto Rico has three such bays, including one in Fajardo and another on Vieques. Culebra, too, has a bay that often exhibits bioluminescence, but not as reliably as the other three.

"The ecosystem in La Parguera is very similar to what we'll see on Culebra," says Francisco. "It's surrounded by semi-arid hills; the waters are clear and shallow. There are mangroves everywhere, healthy seagrass beds, patch reefs, fringing reefs, barrier reefs. So when we go to Culebra you'll feel like you've been there before. And you'll know what we're looking for."

As I plan the trip across the island, I decide to make it a family affair. Sonia has relatives in Ponce, which is en route, as well as in Sabana Grande, just inland of La Parguera. It's time to take the wee one, baby Brett, to visit his extended family.

Horns toot, radios blare as we join the great convoy driving south on Highway 1, the old road to Ponce. We share the road with monstrous Fords and Chevys and Buicks, vintage 1950s models with gaudy grills and sweeping tail fins. Many are hand painted baby blue or shocking pink or vivid lemon. Weaving among them are odd little Euro cars that look like cartoon characters or something out of the novelty song "Beep Beep." Foam dice and prayer cards dangle from rearview mirrors, hula girls bobble on dashboards. Bumpers, fenders, and even windshields are plastered with stickers: *Puerto Rico me encanta*— Puerto Rico enchants me, *Me jodió la telefónica*—I was fucked by the telephone company, and *Como no explican?*—Why don't they explain these things? Road signs are in Spanish, but since they are universally ignored I haven't felt the need to learn what they mean, with the notable exceptions of *CARRETERA CERRADA*, road closed; *PELIGRO*, danger; and *DESPRENDIMIENTO*, landslide. These seem worth knowing.

Highway 1 leads past miles of suburban sprawl. The *urbanizaciones* consist of identical cement boxes in light pastels. Every window is barred. These are Puerto Rico's Levittowns (one is actually called Levittown), and they are sprouting up all over greater San Juan. The signs of a burgeoning consumer society are everywhere: Walgreens, Midas Muffler, Burger King. We pass a salvage yard filled with old cars and appliances stacked impossibly high, and above it all a huge billboard that reads, *YUNK*.

Eventually the highway climbs up through a high pass in the central highlands, the Cordillera Central, a ridge of mountains that runs almost sixty miles from east to west, bisecting the island. The northern slopes receive the full bounty of moisture from the northeast trade winds, while the southern slopes are relatively arid. On our descent, there's a spectacular view of the coastal plain and the Caribbean Sea beyond. The waters are like bands of jewels. Radiating out to sea are concentric arcs of tourmaline, emerald, aquamarine, sapphire.

We turn off the main road and head west. A two-lane road leads through sugarcane fields. We stop at a roadside stand that sells sugarcane juice. An old black woman in a head scarf pours cane juice into paper cups. It is so potent I worry it will dissolve whatever enamel is left on my teeth. And if the juice doesn't do the job, the sticks of sugarcane will. She sells them by the bundle, the cane stripped of the hard outer rind and quartered. They're meant to be not eaten but chewed, one's mouth and jaws serving as a kind of sugar mill to extract the juices, though one can't help but swallow some slivers. It's like consuming sweetened splinters.

An oxcart rolls past, laden with cane. A half dozen men follow, wearing straw hats and rubber boots and carrying machetes. The men are more *café negro* than *café con leche*, as they say—more black coffee than coffee with milk. It's a legacy of the slave trade that supplied the burgeoning sugar industry in the eighteenth century. The skin color of the populace varies with the altitude—the higher, the lighter. The small farms in the mountains didn't demand slave labor.

The road winds through rolling foothills past groves of oranges, avocados, and plantains. Plantain trees, with their big floppy leaves, are grown everywhere in the mountains. The banana-like fruits are eaten green or ripe. They're sliced, diced, mashed, or left whole; fried, baked, boiled, or grilled. Picked while still unripe, plantains leave green stains on the clothes and hands. The mark of a true *jíbaro*, Adair once told me, is *la mancha del platano*—the stain of the plantain.

And we are now entering *jíbaro* country. While the origin of the word *jíbaro* is unclear—in Cuba it means "wild dog"—it is often translated as "hillbilly" or "mountain peasant." But perhaps this does the *jíbaro* an injustice. The poet Manuel Alonzo described the *jíbaro* as "humane, affable, just, and generous." Once considered country bumpkins and subjected to ridicule, the *jíbaros* are now idealized as representing the very soul of Puerto Rico.

We drive under cathedral arches of bamboo that loom over the road. African tulip trees are in bloom, as are the flame trees with their brilliant red-orange flowers. They leave a carpet of fiery red petals on the road. Small general stores and little cafés are built where the road curves around the hillsides. They have names like *Bar El Coquí, Pucho's Place, Gato Perdido* (Lost Cat). Wooden houses in faded blue, green, pink, or yellow sit close to the road. It's siesta time, and country folk are relaxing on their porches. Men are dozing in wooden rockers, their straw hats tipped over their eyes. Women are sewing patches on clothes, keeping one eye out for half-naked children playing hide-and-go-seek in the tobacco fields. Their skin is the golden brown of tobacco leaves drying in the sun.

At a half mile up, Aibonito is the highest town in Puerto Rico. Aibonito—*ay qué bonito!*—how beautiful! These words were supposed to have been uttered by the first Spaniard to set eyes on the place. It's a little jewel of a town set in a ring of stunning mountains. The twin steeples of San José Church overlook a plaza dotted with trees shaped like Magritte umbrellas. There's also a movie theater, now playing *Barbarella*. A movie poster trumpets "the space-age adventuress whose sex-ploits are among the most bizarre ever seen." Jane Fonda, clad in a skimpy futuristic elf costume and armed with a ray gun, peers out from the poster, over the nineteenth-century plaza. The plaza is empty under the midday sun, and we drive around it looking for the spoke to the main road. We end up on a serpentine road that climbs steeply up into La Cordillera, and edges out over deep ravines.

The road skirts San Cristóbal Canyon, some five miles long. Turkey vultures float on updrafts from the Río Usabón, seven hundred feet below. Kestrels sit on their nests in the gnarled gray walls of the crevasse. Somewhere near here, the last skirmish of the Spanish-American War was fought, on August 25, 1898, when a handful of Spanish soldiers tossed stones at a US Navy patrol that was wandering, lost, in the mountains. Fought "on Puerto Rican time," the battle took place the day after armistice was signed.

Trees and telephone poles have been plastered with Marlboro and Coca Cola signs and posters from the PDP—the Popular Democratic Party, or *populares*. The posters feature the party's symbol, the profile of a *jíbaro* in a big straw hat.

The PDP—the pro-commonwealth party—was founded by Puerto Rico's first native-born governor, Luis Muñoz Marín, from the mountain town of Barranquitas. He governed the island from 1949 to 1965, and he's worshipped up here. In the English-language newspaper the *San Juan Star,* a political cartoon depicted Muñoz as God in the Michelangelo painting, reaching down from the heavens to touch the hand of his successor, Governor Roberto Sánchez Vilella. Muñoz Marín, a fiery orator and political populist, was also something of a poet:

> I have broken the rainbow
> against my heart
> as one breaks a useless sword against a knee. . . .

In his later years, Muñoz Marín spoke of the need for *serenidad*—serenity—as a worthy political cause. The need to create a Puerto Rico "where the spirit of man is nurtured by a passionate wish to be free, rather than a passionate wish to be a possessor." Here in his mountains I think I know what he was talking about. It's the serenity that comes from being disengaged from the madness of it all.

A tortuous road leads us south again toward the sea. When we reach the coast, we rejoin Highway 1 heading west. Here the road hugs the coastline, cutting through green cactus and gray scrub and golden grasses. The cloudless sky is desert blue. Vultures hover. Except for glimpses of the sea, it looks like the American Southwest.

Soon we are in the city of Ponce and circling La Plaza de Las Delicias, the plaza of delights. The plaza is graced with walkways of rose-hued stone, gnarled fig trees, and a central fountain guarded by water-spewing lions. Architectural oddities abound. There's a cathedral with twin steeples that look like fire hydrants with portholes. Fittingly, it is next to the firehouse, the Parque de Bombas, which itself is a riot of quirky features. With red and black horizontal bands, half-moon windows, and tulip-shaped hanging lamps, it's like something out of a chil-

dren's storybook. There's also a bank building that looks like a
Greek temple built for Athena. And a hotel featuring Egyptian
friezes like those found on the tomb of King Tut.

The grand houses in the surrounding neighborhood also
are eclectic in style. There's a Roman villa, a Spanish hacienda,
a Southern mansion, a Russian *dacha*, an English manor, a
White House, a French whorehouse.

Ponce was once the main port for the great sugar and coffee
plantations of the south coast. If San Juan was the political and
cultural center for the conservative Spanish elite, Ponce was the
vibrant *rive gauche* for the creoles. It was here during the Spanish colonial era that the movement for autonomy took hold.

Dr. Ramón Betances was an early leader of Puerto Rico's
independence movement. In *The Puerto Ricans,* Kal Wagenheim and Olga Jimenez de Wagenheim quote a broadside that
he is believed to have written:

> For more than three centuries Spanish despotism has op-
> pressed us. . . . For more than three centuries, we have been
> paying immense taxes, and still we have no roads, railways,
> telegraph systems, or steamships. . . . The *gíbaros* are poor
> and ignorant because of the Government, which prohibits
> schools, newspapers, and books. . . . *Arriba* Puerto Ricans!
> Let us . . . rise en masse against the oppressors.

In 1886, Puerto Rican separatists gathered in Ponce and
issued a declaration demanding autonomy from Spain. In response, the Crown sent General Romualdo Palacio González
to govern the island. He quickly instituted his own Inquisition.

Hundreds of creoles were imprisoned and tortured, some to death. It was Puerto Rico's Year of the Terror.

But the repressive measures instilled in the people an even greater desire for freedom. A new Autonomy Party was created by Román Baldorioty de Castro, who had led the successful fight for the abolition of slavery on the island. He was joined by the poet-statesman José de Diego, who wrote:

Resurge, breathe, cry, walk, fight,
vibrate, undulate, thunder, shine.
Do as the river with the rain: grow!
and as the sea against the rock: strike!

When the Liberals in Spain assumed power in 1898, Puerto Rico was granted autonomy at last. It adopted a democratic form of government with two legislative houses. Elated and charged with anticipation, the legislators met for the first time on July 8, 1898. It was also the last time they would meet. Just a few weeks later, a force of sixteen thousand American troops landed at Guánica Bay on the banks of the Río Loco, the Crazy River.

We pull up to an elegant stucco house with a roof of Roman tile and arched windows draped with old-growth bougainvillea. At the dark-mahogany door, we're greeted by Sonia's great aunts, Juana and Clara. Juana says she's sorry that her husband Felipe is not here to greet us. He's working today at the bakery. But there is someone, says Clara, who will love to see you and especially love to see *el nene.*

Juana and Clara lead us into the room of Doña Inés. Doña Inés is Brett's great-great grandmother. She is 106 years old.

The old woman is lying in a small four-poster bed that's shrouded with fine mesh netting. I can barely make out her features through the gauze. She's wearing a high-collared night-dress and has her hair in a bun. She is frail, tiny, and ghostly white.

"*Doña Inés,*" says Aunt Juana. "*Mira, quienes están!*" Look who is here. "*Sonia y su marido y su nene. Y su nene Brett.*" The aunts prop up Doña Inés with pillows so she can better see the baby.

"*Mira, qué guapo es!*" says Juana. Look how handsome he is.

"*Qué guapo,*" echoes Doña Inés in a faint, quivering voice.

"*Tan grande también,*" says Aunt Juana. So big too.

"*Tan grande también,*" whispers Doña Inés.

I wonder if at age 106 she's only capable of repeating what's said to her. Still, I'm awed to be in the presence of someone whose own history reaches back into the nineteenth century.

"Do you think she remembers when the Americans first came to Puerto Rico?" I ask the aunts.

"She was already a young woman," says Aunt Juana. "Ponce was the first city the American soldiers came through. She would have seen the big parade."

I can imagine Doña Inés in a prim white dress, long-sleeved with a high Victorian collar, watching from the balcony of this very house as the US Army's First Division marched by. Flags of every nation adorned the buildings of Ponce. Every nation but Spain, that is. In the carriage of honor, General Nelson

Miles and General Henry Wilson waved to the onlookers. Did she wave back?

"*Doña Inés,*" says Sonia, "*recuerda cuando llegaron los americanos a Puerto Rico.*" Do you remember when the Americans arrived in Puerto Rico?

"*Cuando llegaron los americanos,*" repeats Doña Inés. Then her voice trails off.

"I think it may be time for Doña Inés to take her nap," says Aunt Juana.

But then the old woman pipes up again: "*Cuando llegaron los americanos . . . les tiramos flores . . .*" When the Americans first came, we threw them flowers.

Her frail hand makes a slow tossing motion.

The Spanish-American War in Puerto Rico was called a moonlight picnic. There was little resistance, the Spaniards retreating deeper into the mountains with only the occasional skirmish. In most towns and villages the Americans were welcomed with open arms; the local authorities were eager to capitulate. Most notable was the surrender of the town of Juana Díaz to Stephen Crane, author of *The Red Badge of Courage*. Covering the war for the Hearst papers, he had wandered into town while exploring the countryside. The town fathers immediately placed Juana Díaz under his command. For three days he was treated like the town mayor.

Meanwhile, on the north coast, a fleet of American ships appeared off San Juan. The fleet commander was Admiral William T. Sampson, who had suffered a humiliating experience in the war in Cuba. He had been away at a meeting while his

subordinate, Commodore Schley, led the fleet into an important naval battle at Santiago Bay. Schley was acclaimed a hero,
so popular they even named a pecan after him. Sampson, on
the other hand, was roundly ridiculed. Thomas Edison made
a docudrama—one of the first ever made—in which Schley
is shown on the bridge, heroically directing the ships' guns in
battle, while Sampson is entertaining a group of old ladies at
an afternoon tea party.

Admiral Sampson hoped to salvage his reputation with a
bold attack on San Juan. This time *he* would be on the bridge
directing fire. At 5:00 a.m. sharp, his fleet of iron ships took
aim at the fortress El Morro. With the new rifled cannons, the
enormous citadel of stone was nigh impossible to miss. Yet miss
they did. An unusual confluence of wind and tide and current
had produced the kind of sea described in ships' logs as "con-
fused." The ships lurched this way and that, as did the guns
and crews. Shells soared over the fort, and fell here and there
on the sleeping city. Homes, shops, and churches were struck.
One errant shell cracked the walls of the insane asylum, liberat-
ing its inmates; they ran through the streets rejoicing. In those
days, an attack without warning on a civilian population was
considered contemptible, even cowardly. The luckless Admiral
Sampson was universally condemned for the assault. He sailed
from the island under another cloud of ignominy.

In the end, only seven Americans and a few dozen Spaniards lost their lives in the invasion.

"It wasn't much of a war," said Theodore Roosevelt, "but it
was all the war there was."

CHAPTER 12
Luminous Spirits

O World, all is night,
life is the lightning.
        —Octavio Paz, "Live interval"

We resume our journey west along the south coast and soon come to Guayanilla Bay, a fine natural harbor. It is narrow and very deep and angled to the sea, an excellent hurricane hole. It now serves as a tanker port, surrounded by acres of refineries and petrochemical plants. Guayanilla is a grim-looking place: futuristic towers spew multi-colored fumes into a pewter sky. The acrid smell of sulfur is in the air. Through the pastel haze, one sees a tangle of steel pipes and tanks. A lifeless anomaly. Commonwealth Oil has a plant here, as does Dow Chemical, the manufacturer of napalm and Agent Orange.

A bit further west is Guánica Bay, site of the American invasion. A stone monument commemorating the event has been placed here by the Daughters of the American Revolution. Further out in the bay lies the rusting hulk of the SS *Daniel Pierce*, which ran aground on a sandbar. Spray painted on its side are the words *Su Patria o su Muerte*. Homeland or Death.

The southwest coast with its many coves and cays was pirate country. During the Spanish colonial period, the daily lives of the vast majority of Puerto Ricans had little connection with official proclamations, laws, and regulations. The creoles sought, and mostly found, freedom from supervision by Spanish authorities. By virtue of their numbers, the creoles made their own rules.

When the mother country, Spain, failed to bring trade to the island, the creoles created their own trade. The "men of the other band" called it smuggling, and it was outlawed. But timber, cattle, hides, ginger, and tobacco from the island were freely exchanged for clothing, wine, and tools brought by foreign merchant ships.

"There is an open contraband trade throughout the island," wrote Governor Alejandro O'Reilly, an Irish emigré brought in as a kind of efficiency expert. "The foreign ships come without bothering to hide their intentions, they drop anchor in any port, send their launch or canoe ashore, the inhabitants flock to the beach, and there the business is done."

The incidence of smuggling was so high that the punishment for it—the death penalty—could not be applied, "because to stop such a trade by means of such punishment," wrote one cleric to the King, "would be for Your Majesty to be left without Subjects on the whole island."

Spain's solution to the smuggling problem was to encourage Puerto Ricans to raid *foreign* vessels suspected of illicit trade. To fight smuggling with piracy. *In History of Puerto Rico: A Panorama of its People,* Fernando Picó tells of one such pirate, Pedro de la Torre, who after countless successful attacks on the ships of Spain's enemies was audacious enough to request a knighthood from the Cabildo in Spain. But the royal commissioners found "that all the necessary circumstances for declaring nobility are lacking and that the said don Pedro is not . . . legitimate." In short, he was a creole bastard and certainly not worthy of knighthood.

Supporting creole piracy soon backfired on Spain, most notably in the person of the dashing Roberto Cofresí. He raided English, Dutch, and French ships, yes, but then in an admirable display of initiative he raided Spanish ships as well. These were laden with gold and silver from Spain's other colonies and were far more lucrative. Yet despite his enterprising spirit, Cofresí was captured and tried and shot.

I can imagine Cofresí's argument in his defense. Raiding Spanish ships is wrong? *Como no explican?* Why don't they explain these things? It's the most ubiquitous saying on the island; it's seen on T-shirts, bumper stickers, and billboards, and heard as punch lines on television shows and tag lines in radio commercials. *Como no explican?* It's not my fault; it's the system, *coño.* And for more than five hundred years, Puerto Ricans have been bucking the system.

We take a narrow side road that leads from Guánica to Parguera. The southwest corner is the most arid part of the island. Parched hills are dotted with mesquite and cacti, scrawny goats, and cattle. Salt pans glisten like a sea of diamonds under the brutal sun.

The village of Parguera has only been around since the 1940s. The Spaniards, convinced that the unearthly glow of its waters were the work of the devil, avoided the place. And so it lacks the Spanish colonial charm of other towns and villages in Puerto Rico. The town square is simply that: a paved square in the center of town. It is surrounded by fast-food kiosks featuring the usual fare of codfish fritters, fried plantains, and stuffed potato balls. Thanks to the Phosphorescent Bay, tourism has replaced fishing as the locals' primary source of income. Souvenir stands offer bleached-white corals, seashell knickknacks, and T-shirts. One T-shirt features a picture of a naked woman with a shocked expression on her face, and the line, "*Ay Dios mio!* It glows in the dark!"

Sonia drops me off at the Parguera public pier. She and Brett will venture on to Sabana Grande for a visit with another set of great-grandparents. Longevity is the norm in Puerto Rico.

The pier is lined with brightly painted fishing skiffs, dive boats, and canopied tour boats that will depart in the evening for the bioluminescent waters. The harbor is crowded with small sailboats, yachts, and cruisers at anchor. Along the shoreline in either direction, nestled among the mangroves, are *casitas*, small vacation houses built on public waters. Most are on stilts, but others float on massive pontoons. Their presence here is very controversial. Not only have they displaced crucial habitat but their domestic waste flows directly into the bay, a unique ecosystem and one of the most fragile in Puerto Rico.

It's one of life's paradoxes that man's appreciation of places of natural beauty often leads to the denigration or destruction of those very same places. Awed by the magnificence of Yosemite Falls, we build a luxury hotel and restaurants and parking lots for an endless stream of visitors by car, and "campsites" for countless motor homes. Dazzled by the majesty of the Grand Canyon, we soar up and down a Natural Wonder of the World in helicopters that emit noxious fumes and obnoxious noises. Inspired by the view of sun-dappled barrier islands, we construct walls of high-rise condominiums that darken the beaches with their shadows. Yes, we love Nature. Love it to death.

I make my way to a solitary dock where a sign reads *Laboratorio Departamento de Ciencias Marinas Isla Magueyes.* A green metal cage encloses the dock to discourage casual visitors. But it has not deterred the half dozen Cuban iguanas who claim the dock as their own private lounge area. These are not small creatures. Some are about three feet long, and they range in color from brick red to olive green. One of them glares at me with golden eyes.

Isla Magueyes is just offshore, mere spitting distance from the dock. It's a small, arid island encircled by mangroves. Several research vessels are anchored in a quiet cove. A little jon boat putters over, and a slight man in shorts and flip-flops nudges the boat up to the head of the dock.

"*A la isla?*" he shouts.

"*Sí.*"

"I am Rogilio."

"*Mucho gusto.*"

"Come."

I hop aboard for the sixty-second ride to Isla Magueyes. We tie up across from the *Medusa*, a converted shrimp boat that is the university's main research vessel. Rogilio usually works as the *Medusa*'s mate and is only filling in for his friend, the boat taxi driver. I catch a glimpse of the *Medusa*'s skipper. He's a big, surly looking gringo. Shaved head, scars, tattoos. He might be a pirate king. Now he's cussing up a storm at no one in particular.

I approach a woman in her twenties who is tending to small sharks in an outdoor aquarium. Viola is a graduate student at UPR or "you pee" as the students call it. We chitchat for a while, and she tells me about the shark studies. They're not actually studying the sharks but the little cleaner fish, the wrasses that dart in and out of the sharks' mouths.

"You know how you go to the *dentista* to get your teeth cleaned?" says Viola. "That's what the little fish do. They clean the shark's teeth and mouth. Peck, peck, peck. Leftover food and parasites as well. So the shark gives them a free meal."

"But don't the sharks ever make a meal of the cleaner fish?"

"We shall see," she says with a devilish smile. I'm reminded of a poem by Herman Melville about pilot fish swimming with a great white shark:

> They have nothing of harm to dread,
> But liquidly glide on his ghastly flank
> Or before his Gorgonian head;
> Or lurk in the port of serrated teeth
> In white triple tiers of glittering gates,

And there find a haven when peril's abroad,
An asylum in jaws of the Fates!

I ask Viola if she knows the whereabouts of Jorge Gonzales-Luna, Francisco's contact.

"I saw Jorge earlier today. He might be in the wet lab."

The research station inhabits a cluster of buildings on the island. There are wet and dry labs, indoor and outdoor aquaria, hatchery ponds, classrooms, research libraries, and reference collections of fish, invertebrates, and marine plants and algae. The goal of its charismatic director, Dr. Máximo Cerame-Vivas, is to make the institute a premiere marine research program. By all accounts, he is well on his way to succeeding.

The wet lab is a maze of sinks, tanks, tubes, pumps, and piping. It's rank with the pungent smell of the preservative formalin. One researcher—tall, sandy haired, a gringo perhaps—is pressing fronds of seagrasses into a scrap book. Another man, full-bearded and intense looking, is using tweezers to sort plankton on a tray. Sitting across from him is a Chinese woman in her early thirties, peering into a microscope. Unlike the other grad students, who sport cutoffs, T-shirts, and flip-flops, she wears a long gray dress that reaches from chin to ankles. She's also wearing the high laced boots of a frontierswoman. She looks like a Chinese Mennonite who's misplaced her bonnet.

I ask aloud to no one in particular if Jorge Gonzales-Luna is here.

The Chinese woman looks up and smiles politely. "No. Sorry."

"I think he's up at the lookout area," says the student with the seagrass fronds. "There's a path that will lead you there. You can't miss it."

I follow a steep path that winds past cacti, lignum vitae, and magueys, the tall, spiked century plants that give Isla Magueyes its name. Brown pelicans fly in formation overhead. Cuban iguanas scurry about. I stop for a moment, take a swig of water, and suddenly get the feeling that I'm being watched. And I am. He's up in a twisted, stunted tree, staring at me with big mahogany eyes. His pink face is shaped like a figure eight and framed with bristly cinnamon hairs. And now he's scowling at me, this monkey. He barks loudly, then emits a long, undulating scream.

I have a thing about monkeys. I know we share a common ancestor and all. And I have no problem with Disney monkeys. But real monkeys, monkeys in the flesh, freak me out. Chalk it up to youthful trauma. In the rural Hudson Valley town where I grew up was a general store owned by the Oliverios, a warm and generous Italian-American family. They kept a pet monkey in a cage just outside the store. Every time I'd pass the cage, Bello the monkey would fix me with the most malevolent of looks, unleash a series of shrilly chatters, then masturbate furiously. I was ten or eleven, maybe. Didn't even know the facts of life. But the beast put the fear of the unknown in me. And there you have it. The dark confessional passage that every contemporary memoir seems to require. Sexually harassed by a monkey.

And now its belligerent fellow simian on Isla Magueyes is joined by another, then another, and they're all screeching at me. I hurry on up the hill.

The view from the lookout area is stunning. There are some thirty mangrove islets in the bay, emerald jewels set in a turquoise sea. I had half expected to find Jorge peering through a telescope at a distant school of dolphins or something. But no, there he is: a heavy-set, bespectacled young man snoozing in a hammock, a bound research paper in his lap. He seems lost to the world. I'm not sure if I should wake him or not, but there are those monkeys again, chattering at me, and I might need some backup.

I touch his shoulder, and he sits up with a start.

"Sorry," I say. "Jorge?"

"*Sí, sí.*"

I apologize again for waking him and introduce myself as Francisco's friend.

"Ah, *sí,*" he says. "Francisco Torrejón. He was my mentor. *Buena gente.*" Good people.

He tells me he was working until late last night taking plankton samples in the bay. And he has another long night ahead of him. He notices me glancing nervously at the monkeys.

"They are rhesus monkeys," he says. "But they don't belong here on the island. They escaped from Isla Cueva where they were used for research. We're trying to get rid of them."

"I see."

"You don't like monkeys."

"Well . . ."

"I don't either."

As we descend the hill, Jorge curses back at them in Spanish. Something about their mothers' hairless butts. I like this guy.

In the office of the grad lab, Jorge spreads out a chart of La Parguera on the table.

"The ecosystem is similar to what you'll find on Culebra. The interior is very dry, as I'm sure you noticed, and there are no streams or rivers. Which means very little freshwater runoff. A shallow shelf extends for miles out to sea. We have bays, enclosed and protected like those on Culebra. And mangroves, along all the shores and on all these small islands in the bays. The mangroves filter what little water seeps down from the hills. And they clean the water in the bay as well. Filtered water allows sunlight to penetrate right to the bottom, which helps with the photosynthesis of seagrasses and coral algae. The mangroves also provide habitat and nesting sites for many species of birds, and the bird droppings provide nutrients. Add nutrients and sunlight to clear shallow water and you have an ideal environment for seagrasses. Which is what I'm studying. Seagrasses. As an indicator species of a healthy inshore ecosystem."

"What about bioluminescence? That should be an indicator too, right?"

"In La Parguera, *sí*. It's an excellent gauge of the health of the bay. But there are very few places in the world, six or seven perhaps, where the bioluminescence is permanent enough to serve as an indicator. In Culebra, for example, there's a place called Pelá Bay. Here, I'll show you."

He rolls up the Parguera chart and spreads out a chart of Culebra.

"This is Pelá Bay, here on the eastern end of the island. See the hills surrounding it? Very arid. So the waters remain clear. And look how narrow the entrance is. That keeps the tides from carrying the nutrients out to sea. And there are mangroves all around the shoreline. All the elements for a healthy population of *Pyrodinium bahamense*. That's the plankton that gives off the light. But the bay is only bioluminescent on certain nights. We don't know why."

"Have you ever been there?"

"To Culebra, yes, but to Pelá Bay, no. The Navy has signs up everywhere. *Prohibido pasar!* And these patrol boats chase you off if you try to enter the bay from the sea. But I would love to go. They say the shallows are fields of turtle grass. So, yes, there is bioluminescence on Culebra but it is not as reliable or as impressive as what we have here in Parguera. And what we have here is not as impressive as what they have on Vieques, in Bahía Mosquito, which is *estupenda!* But also ruled off-limits by the Navy. Anyway, if you wish, tonight you can see the light show for yourself. We'll be conducting plankton trawls in the bay from about nine to about eleven. You are welcome to join us."

Later, I grab a quick meal at one of the kiosks in the square: whole red snapper deep fried in a barrel of oil. It's the fish for which La Parguera is named. Then I savor a Corona on the pier and watch the sun drop like a golden Spanish doubloon beyond a distant shore. When it's gone, the stars burst from the sky almost at once. It's the requisite moonless night. I venture over to the marine station dock, where the iguanas welcome me with a look that says, "Oh, you again." A few minutes later, Jorge nudges a Boston Whaler up to the dock. And Viola beckons me from the bow.

"*Buenas noches!* Come, come. Just jump in the boat and let's go! Vroom-vroom!"

Viola, whom I'd met at the shark tank, is from the mountains of Puerto Rico. She has the tawny skin, raven-black hair, and high cheekbones of a Taíno Indian. She loves to embellish her sentences with sound effects. The word "onomatopoeia" comes to mind.

So vroom-vroom we go. Already the waters are luminous in our wake. Jorge takes it slow so we can catch glimpses of life below the surface. Viola leans far out over the bow, looking like the carved figurehead of an Indian maiden.

"*Mira!* Look!" she shouts, and points to a large manta ray gliding above the turtle grass beds. It glows eerily, like an alien spaceship. Other fish dart here and there in bursts of blue-green light.

The phenomenon of bioluminescence remained a mystery for long centuries. In 1688 the Jesuit explorer Pere Guy Tachard offered the following theory: "We attribute the cause to the heat of the sun, which has, as it were, impregnated and filled the sea during the day with an infinity of fiery and luminous spirits. These spirits, after dark, reunite to pass out in a violent state."

In fact, the luminescence is created by nothing more than tiny plankton called dinoflagellates. There are more than seven hundred thousand *Pyrodinium bahamense* per gallon of seawater. Each one is no more than a five hundredth of an inch long. Seen through a microscope, it has the appearance of two horseshoe crab shells pressed together. It is propelled by a pair of whip-like flagella. But how does it generate light? Jorge explains the process to me. The intensity of the flash depends on how much sunlight there was the previous day, and therefore how much photosynthesis occurred. The generating of the flash itself is rather complicated. It has something to do with the chemicals luciferin and luciferase (named after Lucifer!) and their reaction with oxygen and salt. This chemical reaction is triggered when the *Pyrodinium* feels pressure against its cell wall. The burst of light happens almost instantaneously and lasts only a tenth of a second. I never did very well in high school chemistry. Slept through most of the lectures, in fact. My teacher, Mr. Colin Denier, was a guest lecturer from England who simply read his notes verbatim and in the most monotone of British accents. He ended every lecture with an exclamatory "Rrrrright!" And the sound of that one word would wake me.

Which is why I prefer Viola's explanation better: "It's like an explosion of little *bombas*. And they—wheeesh!—light up the sea!"

But *why* do they generate light? No one knows for sure. One theory is that the flash of light is intended to frighten off predators. This seems to make sense since it's only emitted when the water is stirred. But who knows? Maybe they're simply announcing to the world, "Hey folks, we may be tiny, but we're here too!"

Tonight we'll be conducting surface trawls using a long, narrow, cone-shaped net with a collecting cup at its end. Our first collecting transect will be on a line between two mangrove islets. The tide is going out, so we run the line toward the shore. Viola pays out the net as the boat putters slowly through the narrow channel. I take Viola's spot on the bow to watch out for floating debris. Mangrove islands are spooky enough anyway, but they are especially so on a dark night like this one, with these eerie lights flashing in the tangled mangrove roots.

Once we pass through the channel, Jorge cuts the engine and Viola pulls in the net. Like a blue-green phantom, the net disappears and reappears with her every tug. She hauls the net aboard, and water sprinkles on the deck like fairy dust. She unscrews the collecting cup and pours its sparkling contents into a jar. The luminescent plankton are mixed in with other species, Jorge says, and they will be sorted out later.

"It's very time consuming," Viola says. "You need patience. Which I don't have. I'm more like—duh-duh-duh—just picking and sorting. And the smell of the formalin is—fwoof!—it gives me a headache."

"That's why we give the job to Carlito. His mind is always elsewhere. Like on the revolution."

Carlito must be the surly looking guy with the beard.

"I think he's making bombs in his head while he is sorting plankton," says Viola. "'Oh, look here: a copepod,' he says. But in his head, he's thinking, 'kaboom!'"

We move closer to shore for the next run, but the luminescence here has lost some of its brilliance. The lights from the countless shacks lining the mangroves certainly don't help.

"I think that's what Carlito should be blowing up," says Jorge. "Those squatter shacks. *Puñeta!* All their *mierda,* their shit, goes right into the water. That's the one good thing about the Navy in Culebra. Someone builds a shack like that and—boom!—they'll blow the *pendejo* away."

"Maybe we should give La Parguera to the Navy," says Viola facetiously.

In a way, she may be right. The Navy is certainly wreaking havoc on Culebra's environment. But on the other hand, what would happen to the islands if they were to leave? Could things actually get worse? Would Culebra fall victim to rampant and unregulated development? Mangroves cleared for squatter shacks? Hills dotted with condos instead of flame trees? Coral reefs fished out? Nothing is ever simple when it comes to the environment. Nothing is black and white, try as we might to see things that way. And there's no sense in demonizing anyone. "We have met the enemy and he is us," as Pogo said.

It's now past eleven, and we run our last line just offshore of the mangroves almost to the barrier reefs. The water is exceptionally brilliant out here.

"*Eso es!*" says Jorge when Viola pours the last scintillating sample into its jar. That's it!

"*Fua!*" exclaims Viola. Then she pulls her T-shirt over her head, unzips her shorts, strips down to her panties, and shouts, "*Mira!* Watch!"

How could we not?

And she dives into the waters. Her body is immediately encircled in a stunning aura of light. And now she floats on her back and extends her arms and legs and moves them through the glowing waters as a Northern child would move through powdery snows, creating—

"A snow angel! See?" shouts Viola. "*Qué rico, eh?* A snow angel in Puerto Rico!"

And that's exactly what she is.

"Come on, *caballeros!* Don't be shy! Jump in!"

And we do. We plunge into the deliciously warm waters of a star-filled sea. My limbs are instantly aglow. I sweep my hand through the water and leave the trail of a fiery comet. And as we move through the astral liquid our glittering bodies assume fantastic other-worldly shapes.

We are luminous spirits.

CHAPTER 13

Deviation

The sole cause of a man's unhappiness is that he does not know how to stay quietly in his own room.
—Pascal *Pensées, 136*

On our return to San Juan we hear of an extraordinary event. Marisol Malaret Contreras, a willowy beauty born in the mountain town of Utuado, has been named Miss Universe. San Juan has erupted in Marisol Mania.

Marisol is a tall, green-eyed secretary whose story is like something out of *Simplemente María*, or as Delila puts it, "She is our own Cinderella." She was orphaned at the age of ten, after her father suffered a fatal heart attack and her mother passed away months later. Marisol and her elder brother Tony, an invalid, went to live with their Aunt Ester, a kindly old woman who eked out a living selling lottery tickets. "Marisol never gave me any trouble," says Aunt Ester. "She was such a good child."

Marisol won an academic scholarship to UPR's secretarial program. Not long after graduation she got a job with the telephone company. A make-up artist suggested she try some modeling on the side. Soon fashion ads featuring Marisol were appearing in the local publications. When Miss Universe recruiters visited San Juan, the telephone company offered to sponsor Marisol to represent Puerto Rico in the contest. Her poise and polish and warmth won over judges and contestants alike. Her heroes, she said, are God, space, and Werner Von Braun, the rocket scientist. She won the rhinestone crown. The first *puertoriqueña* to do so.

"Her victory," says Governor Ferré, "is a victory for all Puerto Rican women." He calls for a welcome-home parade and a holiday for the government's hundred thousand workers. The parade is the largest in Puerto Rican history and the first ticker-tape parade ever. Thousands greet the new Miss Universe at the airport, tens of thousands line the six-mile route to the capitol building, and hundreds of thousands watch the event on television. The motorcade bearing Marisol passes by to applause and cheers and confetti. Even the penitentiary hangs out a welcoming banner.

"This is the greatest thing that has ever happened to Puerto Rico," says the proprietor of a department store that's crowded with people watching the event on the store's televisions. "We know our women are beautiful. But for one of them to compete with all the greatest nations in the world and to win, why, that's fantastic."

At the capitol building, Marisol is met by the Governor, the heads of the Commonwealth Senate and House, and the island's Chief Justice. From a podium on the capitol steps, Marisol, batting eyelashes the size of Spanish fans, tosses flower blossoms to the roaring crowd and promises to spread "Love Power" around the world.

The celebration goes on for days. Pepe Scotch-tapes magazine photos of Marisol on the walls and scrawls "Love Power" beneath them. The *amigos* gaze at Marisol longingly, and Marisol gazes back at them, her green eyes ringed with dark mascara.

"*La quiero*," says Wilfredo with the dog named Puppy. I love her.

"*Yo también*," says Blanquita. Me too.

Marisol Mania does not end with the parade. Her photos grace countless magazines, newspapers, billboards, and flyers. A new bumper sticker appears: *MARISOL ME ENCANTA.* Marisol enchants me. Poems are written in her honor, as well as countless songs.

She also provides Fredo with a new *piropo.* We are towing the trailer en route to picking up the *Maroho,* and as we pass a *señorita* Fredo coos, "Marisol may have the crown, *nena,* but you have the walk."

The boat's engine has finally been flushed and rebuilt. This time the launching will be a quiet, discreet affair. We'll use the boat ramp at the Cangrejos Yacht Club.

Fredo asks if we can stop by his house to pick up his 35mm camera. He wants to take a photo of the boat. "This is history, man. History." Fredo has been dabbling in many things lately:

still photography, martial arts, marijuana horticulture. He says he's seeking a new direction in life. He attended the University of St. Louis, a Jesuit school. I can't quite imagine Fredo adhering to the strict regimen of the Soldiers of Christ. Neither apparently could he, and he dropped out after his freshman year.

Fredo lives with his parents in El Condado, an oceanfront community just east of Old San Juan. In the early twentieth century Condado was home to wealthy American industrialists. The streets were laid out in 1908 by the Behn Brothers, founders of the Puerto Rico Telephone Company. Condado is now mostly a tourist strip with nightclubs, casinos, boutiques, and fancy restaurants. Most of the major hotels are located here. The Caribe-Hilton is the most lavish—and the most controversial, for its attempt to exclude the locals from its strip of beach. The Condado Beach Hotel, once the winter home of the Vanderbilts, is smaller but more gracious. The Hotel La Concha is notable for its beachfront pavilion shaped like a giant conch shell. This hotel always suffers a shortage of towels and ashtrays and anything else that has *La Concha* imprinted on it. Visiting Latin American tourists treasure these items, as *la concha* is a slang term for "pussy."

Hidden away from the tourist crowd is the oldest part of El Condado, a residential neighborhood with elegant homes that evoke the Spanish colonial era. Fredo's family lives in a rambling stucco mansion with arched windows and Roman-tiled roofs. But there is little in Fredo's attitude or demeanor to suggest a sense of entitlement. If anything, he seems embarrassed by his parents' wealth, and he often rails against the children of the privileged class, the *blanquitos*. "I grew up with the *blan-*

quitos, man. Puerto Rican parents love to spoil their kids, but the rich kids are, like, super spoiled. Anything they want, their parents will buy for them. Speedboats, BMWs, ski trips, even high-class hookers." Fredo himself prefers the simpler life.

As we approach an imposing iron gate, Fredo juggles countless keys until he finds the right one. I can see that the windows are barred, as they are in many Puerto Rican homes. The bars have been shaped and forged by an artisan into a lacy filigree.

An elderly maid greets us at the front door and tells Fredo that his father is still at work and that *la señora* has gone to a luncheon. We enter a parlor lined with oil paintings—mostly portraits of the family—then go through a massive mahogany door that leads to an inner courtyard. It's a green oasis of shade-loving plants. In the center, a stone maiden pours a jug of water into a scalloped basin. Fredo's room is on the far side of the patio.

The room is pure Fredo: shoes and clothes scattered everywhere. "No place to put them," he says. "I turned the closet into a dark room." Martial art sticks are draped over his dresser. "Nunchakus. That's how I got this bump on my head." Black and white photos are Scotch-taped to the walls. They're mostly of female nudes, of course. "*La rubia*, the blonde one, was my girlfriend. She got mad when I took photos of the others." There are also portraits of kids from the barrios. These are quite good. "I let that kid take some pictures with my camera," he says, pointing to a street urchin with a Yankees cap. "Then he dropped it. It's OK. I bought this Leica, which is better."

We go back across the patio into the kitchen, where two chilled glasses of guava juice await us, courtesy of Pilar, the cook. She chides Fredo for drinking it down too fast. *"Despa-cio, m'hijo. Despacio!"*

"These people," he says, "are like family. And I'm still the baby."

"Nene, sí!" Pilar says with a laugh.

The yacht club is nestled in a mangrove-dotted lagoon just east of a popular local beach, Isla Verde. More than 150 power boats are docked here; most are modest in size. A low bridge across the entrance channel to the sea restricts passage to boats with superstructures of less than thirteen feet.

Thankfully, the launching proves uneventful, although once again it takes Fredo a good half hour to align the trailer on the ramp. I check that the boat plug is in. Check it again. Check it once more for good measure. With the boat in the water, I lower the stern drive and crank the starter. The engine turns over without so much as a sputter. Perhaps some of Mari-sol Malaret's can-do spirit has rubbed off on the *Maroho*.

We cruise very slowly just offshore to break in the engine. Still, even at lower rpms, the engine is pretty loud. I lift the engine cover and see there is no baffling on its inner sides. *Ay, cabrón!*

Over the next three days, we slowly cruise up and down the coast on a line parallel to the shore. We head west as far as the mansions of Condado and east as far as the shacks of Piñones. The long public beach between, Playa Isla Verde, is mostly devoid of beachgoers, these being work days. On the weekends, Playa Isla Verde will be crowded. There will be loud music blasting from portable radios and tape decks. And food,

food, food, with smoke from countless grills wafting through the palms. And families wading in the shallows, many of them fully-clothed. But, not a snorkel in sight. And I reflect again on the cautious relationship Puerto Ricans have with the sea.

After a good fifteen hours of engine running time, the *Maroho*'s break-in period is over. It's time to bring her up to full speed. Now the engine noise is deafening. Jesus. Can't hear yourself think. And worse: no matter how much throttle I give the engine, the boat refuses to get up on a plane. This limits her potential speed to her "hull speed." Hull speed is calculated using a formula based on the length of a boat's waterline. Unless a boat can get up on a plane, freeing itself from the water it displaces, its speed is limited by the boat's size. The *Maroho*, at twenty-six feet, will be able to go at only about six knots, not much faster than a brisk walk.

I ask around the marina, and the consensus among other boat owners is that the problem is most likely the diameter or pitch of the propeller. Pitch is the distance a prop moves through water in one revolution. It determines the propeller's bite in the water and thus the speed with which it can propel the boat. It's not unusual for a boat owner to try out propellers of various pitches and diameters to find the one that produces the optimal speed. This can be a time-consuming procedure, but it's worth the effort, especially with a boat that moves at the speed of a sea slug.

Bruno grumbles about providing me with additional propellers. He has yet to be paid for the one that came with the boat. But Fredo tells him that unless we can get the boat up to speed, we won't be able to invite the office girls for a boat ride.

"*Tu sabes,* those *chicas* who wear bikinis the size of postage stamps." A boat ride, Fredo adds, that Bruno is invited to take with us. We leave the boatyard with armloads of propellers.

We haul the boat from our slip at the yacht club and change props. Then we head just offshore and give it full throttle to try to get the boat up on a plane. We spend days testing props, hauling and launching the boat again and again. But the *Marojo* stubbornly refuses to achieve liftoff. The boat plows through the ocean like a garbage scow. It seems we are forever doomed to poking along at six knots.

I decide to abandon the speed trials for now, until I can bring the boat's designer aboard to assess the problem firsthand. Assuming the boat had a designer. Instead I will focus on calibrating the compass. This has been Cruz-Cruz's highest priority. "*Capitán,*" he asks me on a daily basis, "have you calibrated the compass yet?"

"No sir, not yet. Still trying to work out the problems with getting the boat up to planing speed."

"The compass must be calibrated. It is critical."

"OK. Will do."

"It is most critical."

"Yes, sir."

Cruz-Cruz's obsession with the compass is like something out of medieval times, when lodestone, a magnetic ore, was considered to have powers beyond simply pointing north. Ground into a powder and mixed into an elixir of sweetened water, lodestone could cure baldness, gout, and obesity, and even restore youth. Placed under the pillow of an unfaithful wife, it could induce her to confess her crimes in her sleep.

But lodestone could also cause madness. Even standing near a compass for too long could cause one to become disoriented and wander far from family, home, and country. I myself have been so afflicted.

There are two types of compass errors: variation and deviation. Variation is caused by the fact that the magnetic pole is not precisely situated on the geographic north pole. The error varies with geographic location, and in Puerto Rico it's about twelve degrees West. Deviation error is caused by extraneous magnetic forces in the immediate vicinity of the compass. Deviation must be calibrated. You pick two prominent features on the chart, draw a line through them, and determine the true bearing of that line. Then, out in the boat, you cross the line at various angles, taking a compass bearing at the precise moment the two visual markers are aligned. With these bearings you can create a table that gives the deviation for headings at all points of compass. The true course is then calculated using the sailor's memory aid: "True Virgins Make Dull Companions." (That is, the True reading and the Variation error give one the Magnetic reading; add the Deviation error and one gets the Compass reading.)

On the day we're to calibrate the compass, our coworkers from the office show up at the dock. They've generously cleared their busy calendars to assist us in any way possible. Toward that end, Ambrosio brings a fishing pole on board. Gabo brings his meditation beads. Delila, a shopping bag full of food. Mercedes, a bottle of rum. Llorlli, a portable radio, which is blaring a popular song about a joyful day at the beach: "*Chiri biri bi, pom pom pom pom. Chiri biri bi, pom pom pom pom.*"

The owls and the pussycats set out to sea in a pink and orange boat. Delila passes around codfish fritters and deep-fried potato balls, while Ambrosio distributes chilled cans of India beer. We all have to shout to be heard over the deafening roar of the engine. No one seems to mind though, nor do they mind the plodding speed of the boat. Ambrosio says that six knots is ideal for trolling for dorado, kingfish, and jacks. He ties a silver spoon onto his fishing line and casts out beyond the boat's wake. Gabriel sits up on the bow in the lotus position, eyes closed, hands in prayer, like a carved figurehead on a Burmese junk.

On the chart, I draw a pencil line through the airport control tower and the beacon on the Las Marías breakwater. We'll motor across the line on various headings and record the bearings. On any other boat, the helmsman would simply glance down at the compass and take the bearings himself. Unfortunately, on the *Maroho* the compass has been installed on the port side of the bridge console, while the helm is on the starboard side a good five feet away.

When I brought this to Bruno's attention, back in the work shed, he said it was *no problema.* "If you just lean over a little bit you can read it."

"Maybe if I were a giraffe."

"*Una girafa? Hahaha. Ay, no!*" He stretched his body and bent sideways about ninety degrees. "The compass is pointing . . . *al norte.* To the north. *Mas o menos.* You see? *No problema.*"

As I steer us toward our first line, Ambrosio offers to take the bearings. A geologist who's explored unknown terrain, he's very compass savvy. He sets his fishing pole aside and takes up a position behind the compass. Mercedes volunteers to record the bearings in a notebook. I send Fredo up to the bow to keep a lookout for reefs. Then I steer the boat due west, 270 degrees magnetic, toward the Las Marías beacon.

Gabriel stands at Ambrosio's side, mesmerized by the compass. That a great invisible force manifests itself through the dancing of a tiny compass needle is "*una profundidad inmensa,*" he says—an immense profundity. But to Delila and Llorlli it's more like a black art, the compass a voodoo amulet like those sold by gnarly old *santerías* in the Rio Piedras market. Still, they readily join Fredo on the bow and watch in anticipation as the boat approaches the line. "*Listo?*" Ready? they shout. The moment the beacon lines up with the tower they call out, "*Ya! Eso es!*" Gabriel then taps Ambrosio on the shoulder, and Ambrosio takes the bearing and calls it out to Mercedes: "*Marca dos seis cinco!*"—bearing two six five!—and Mercedes dutifully records it. This way, a one-person task becomes a six-person task. Though it might be inefficient, it certainly makes the process more enjoyable.

The weather gods are kind to us, giving us fair skies and a gentle breeze. We take a break from the task at hand, and Ambrosio casts a lure into crystalline waters. Gabriel meditates. Mercedes dozes. I simply study a flock of pelicans that has singled out the *Maroho* for observation, gracefully gliding over us time and time again. And it is simply wonderful to be out here on the boat today. Or as Water Rat says in Kenneth Grahame's *Wind in the Willows*:

There is *nothing*—absolutely nothing—half so much worth doing as simply messing about in boats. . . . In or out of 'em, it doesn't matter. Nothing seems really to matter, that's the charm of it. Whether you get away, or whether you don't; whether you arrive at your destination or whether you reach somewhere else, or whether you never get anywhere at all.

Leave it to the *Maroho* to test that sentiment. As we resume our crossings of the bearing line, the engine sputters and stalls and there's a collective "*Ay nooo!*" from the team. I check the fuel gauge and it still reads full, despite the fact that we've been running the engine for hours.

"Is it possible the fuel gauge is not working?" asks Ambrosio.

"*Es posible que una cabra tenga cuernos?*" says Fredo. Is it possible that a goat has horns?

I uncap the gas tank, feed a line down into it, pull it out, and lo! there's plenty of gas. I crank the starter, but the engine refuses to turn over. Ah, the ignition key. Since it's located nowhere near the toggle starter, I often forget to turn it on. I do so and try again. The engine still refuses to stir.

"I think it is that pump thing," says Fredo. "You know, for the bilge or whatever." Fredo knows less about engines than I do. Where is a chief engineer when you need one?

"Perhaps it is flooded," says Ambrosio. I open the engine cover and remove the air filter, and yes, gas is seeping out of the carburetor.

"We should remove the sparkplugs and clean the excess gasoline from the tips," says Ambrosio. "Do you have a spark plug wrench?"

No. But I do have six boxes of emergency flares, twelve gallons of bottled water, a case of Spam, and an inflatable raft. Why would I need a spark plug wrench?

The boat is dead in the water, rolling slowly in the swells. The team turns green as sea turtles. Mercedes loses her lunch over the side, which sets off a chain reaction. Soon Delila and Llorlli and Gabriel and Fredo are barfing deep-fried fritters into the sea. Ambrosio tries to put a positive spin on it by observing that at least they're providing chum for the fishing.

Now the boat is slowly drifting toward the public beach at Isla Verde. I decide to let the boat drift closer to shore before dropping anchor. In case we have to abandon ship. In case? Of course we'll have to abandon ship. This is, after all, the *Maroho.*

"Sorry, my friends," I say, "but our little cruise is over."

"*Aaaay nooo.*"

Aaaay sí. One by one they climb over the side. Fredo, standing in water up to his hips, steadies them until they get their footing in the sand. Delila is so woozy from *mal de mer* that she has trouble keeping her balance, and as she totters toward the shallows, a big wave sneaks up from behind and knocks her down. Fredo quickly helps her up and she appears to be crying. No, she's laughing, and now everyone's laughing along with her.

Their only concern seems to be leaving Fredo and me on the boat to fend for ourselves. "We can wait here on the beach," says Ambrosio, "until you start the boat."

"No, that's OK. I know you all need to get back to the office."

"We can bring help," says Gabriel. "I can telephone Bruno at the boatyard."

"Bruno is no help. Don't worry, we'll be fine."

"Shall we bring you more food?" Delila asks. She knows of a café just up the road that sells fried chicken and pork chops and plantains.

"I think we're quite full already, *gracias.*"

Reluctantly they take their leave from us. They hike up the beach to the palm-studded park then turn as one to the *Maroho* and wave goodbye. It's as if they're bidding farewell to the *Titanic.* Fortunately for them, the survivors of the *Maroho* tragedy, it's only a short walk to the Cangrejos Yacht Club, where Ambrosio's car is parked.

As for Fredo and me, we sit on the bow of the boat and simply wait. That's what you do when the carburetor's flooded and you have no spark plug wrench. You wait for the excess gasoline to evaporate. And then you try to start the engine again. And if it floods again, you repeat the cycle. And this goes on and on until either the engine starts or you throw yourself into the sea in despair.

I gaze out at a patch of water that's churning with glass minnows desperate to escape unseen predators. Fredo lights up a joint, leans back against a lifejacket, and stares at the clouds.

"You know, *Capitán,*" he says at last, "I think Marisol is *muy simpática.* She is very friendly. And she is a simple person, *tu sabes.* I think she would be happy with a man who likes the simple joys in life. Good food. Good friends. Good *yerba.*" Someone like Fredo, one assumes.

I crank the engine again and again, until with one last pathetic errrr-errrr of the starter the battery is completely and utterly drained. I suppose I should simply go ashore and walk to the yacht club and cajole a fellow boater into giving us a tow back to the dock. But I just don't have it in me right now.

The *Maroho* is beginning to remind me of my little dog Laddie. Laddie, a perky orange beagle, was given to me for Christmas when I was eight years old.

You want to love your first dog, and I so loved Laddie. But Laddie did not love me. He nipped at my heels, drawing blood from my ankles. Whenever I ran around in play, he sank his teeth into my pant cuffs and shook his head violently until I tripped and fell. In the house, he pissed and shit where he pleased, refusing to be trained. I had to clean it up. Laddie is your dog, said my mother, you're the one who wanted the damn thing. Now wipe up that dog crap! Tied up outside in punishment, Laddie would slip out of his collar and run away. I had to search for him. Laddie is your dog, said my father, you're the one who wanted the damn thing. Now get out there and find him! Laddie preferred to run away during lightning storms, snow blizzards, Arctic cold snaps, force nine gales. I wandered all over the countryside calling for him. "Laddie! Laddieeeee!" When darkness fell, I slowly trekked back home—cold, wet, defeated—with nothing on the end of the leash but an empty collar. Laddie, of course, was there to greet me, mocking me with his shrill yelp.

He didn't even have a decent bark.

CHAPTER 14
Rain

It was like a deluge from heaven, and it rattled on the roof of corrugated iron with a steady persistence that was maddening. It seemed to have a fury of its own. And sometimes you felt that you must scream if it did not stop, and then suddenly you felt powerless.

—W. Somerset Maugham, "Rain"

I n the waning days of the rainy season, a tropical wave drifts eastward from the coast of West Africa, passes over the Canaries, and then travels thirteen hundred nautical miles across the Atlantic where it is drawn inexorably into a massive upper level trough over Puerto Rico. There, it stalls. But we pay little mind to weather reports. We have other concerns.

The news regarding Culebra is not good. That is, if you are a Culebran. If you're an Admiral in the Navy the news is very good, indeed. CULEBRA POT BOILS reads the headline of an editorial in the *San Juan Star.* The House subcommittee on Culebra has issued its report. It has determined that the "inconvenience" of range firing on the citizens of Culebra is "infinitesimally small." Further, that the Navy has made an extensive search and has found no site which could substitute for Culebra.

"There have been charges in the press that the Navy cares more for its weapons than for human beings," the report adds. "This subcommittee does not consider this to be the case."

Puerto Ricans both at home and on the US mainland have reacted angrily. In San Juan, more than five hundred demonstrated at the Isla Grande Naval Air Station. They carried placards reading *"Marina Afuera Culebra."* Navy Out of Culebra. On Culebra itself the islanders threatened to storm the Navy's observation post, while some three hundred protesters set up camp in a target zone. In New York, it's Governor Luis A. Ferré who's on the receiving end of the people's wrath. During the Puerto Rico Day Parade, eggs, tomatoes, and oranges were tossed at him by hundreds of demonstrators, while at the parade across the river in Newark, an effigy of the governor was tossed about.

But why take it out on the governor?

"He is *una puta!*" says Pepe. "*Una puta!*" A whore.

"*Una puta de caché!*" adds Ramón. A gold-digging whore.

"*Exacto!*" says Blanquita.

Many feel that in the battle for Culebra, the governor has been a deserter. Or worse: a collaborator. Even the normally accommodating *San Juan Star* takes him to task:

To a government which doesn't want to rock the boat and jam the door to statehood, the Culebra-Navy dispute is an unfortunate nuisance it would be better not to have to reckon with. . . . Ferré has cautiously adopted a conciliatory attitude, shunning commitment in favor of confusion.

The governor never mentions our impending survey of the island. Not that it's a secret. It's already been in the newspaper. But he never speaks of its potential role in resolving the Culebra issue, in stopping the bombing, or even in returning Culebra to the Culebrans. Perhaps he has little faith in our ability to truly accomplish anything. Or little faith in America's newfound commitment to the environment.

In Pepe's Place, the outrage over Culebra mirrors the brewing storm outside. Adaír seems to take it personally. As the rains beat against the windows, he rails against the bombing of Culebra.

"They got islands off Texas, man. Islands off Maine. Islands off Georgia, *carajo!* Why don't they bomb those islands? No, it's easier to fuck the Puerto Ricans. That's what they think. Fuck the Puerto Ricans!"

For Adair—suffering from shrapnel wounds and post-traumatic stress syndrome from his service in Vietnam—the shelling of Culebra has become something personal. The rain is falling more heavily now, and I suggest to him that we head home before it gets worse. He waves me off.

"If it gets worse, this is the only place to be. We have everything we need at Pepe's Place. *Verdad*, Pepe?"

"Everything you need, *hermano*," Pepe says as he tapes up another photo of Marisol on the wall. "And Marisol, too."

I bid adios to the *amigos* and head home in the rain. The clouds are a rippling blanket of tarnished silver; monstrous mammaries hang below them, laden with moisture. The clouds don't appear to be moving. And if they don't move soon . . .

According to the National Weather Service, Puerto Rico has the greatest recurring threat to life and property due to flash flooding of any state or territory. It is also one of the most difficult places to make accurate weather predictions. Tropical waves are continually generated off West Africa—there's one every three to five days—and their paths are notoriously fickle and aimless. Even when their arrival in Puerto Rico is certain, the amount of precipitation is not. There are powerful local influences—water everywhere and a rugged topography—that determine if and when and how much it will rain. By the time a heavy rain event becomes imminent, it's often too late to take preventative action against flash flooding.

This year Puerto Rico has seen more than its share of severe weather events. In June, a foot of rain fell in twenty-four hours in the mountain town of Gurabo. Landslides sent *casitas* tumbling down into the roaring waters of the Rio de Gurabo. River waters then flowed into the urban area of Puerto Nuevo. Thousands evacuated their homes.

In July, torrential rains fell on the marshes of Cucharillas, and the swamp waters oozed out into the surrounding barrios. An elderly couple drowned when they ventured out in search of their lost pig. A few days later, Mother Nature threw in an earthquake for good measure, the worst in fifty years, a forty-five second temblor that *gracias a Dios* killed no one. I was in my office at the time, and sheet rock collapsed all around me and filled the room with billowing clouds of gypsum powder. I emerged from the rubble (it was rubble before the quake) unhurt but looking like a circus clown in whiteface.

In August, flash floods struck yet again, this time in Bayamón, a heavily populated suburb of San Juan set in the foothills of the Cordillera Central. It's a land rife with rivers: the Minillas, the Cuesía, the Guaynabo, the Hondo, the Bayamón. All very vulnerable to flooding. Bayamón is dense with *urbanizaciones,* and many people drowned when the rivers overflowed.

And now, in September, there's the potential for yet another storm from hell, as the locals call them. Sonia and I and the wee one sit on our veranda listening to the rain pounding the aluminum awning like machine-gun fire. Already rivulets are gushing down the streets of Los Maestros. This is a strange storm. There's no thunder or lightning and very little wind. There's only the rising and falling crescendo of the rains. The fluting on the awning channels the rain into streams of water, creating liquid columns that add a touch of ancient Greece to the house. Storm waters have spilled over onto our front lawn. We watch flotsam drift by in an alliterative procession: basketballs, baby dolls, bird nests, beer cans, brassieres.

The power is out. Phone too. On our portable radio, the broadcast is all crackly like those radios in the Depression era. But we can make out the news reports well enough, and by all accounts things are not good. The storm is very widespread, covering the entire eastern two-thirds of the island. Ponce, usually sheltered from storms by the Cordillera Central, has been hit very hard, and the main coastal road has been closed.

All the roads to San Juan have flooded, creating a traffic jam from Arecibo to Fajardo. There's been no official announcement of a government closing, but I know it's pointless to go in to work. No one will be there. Still, I can't help worrying about the *Maroho*. We left it at its dock, and there must be a foot of water in it by now. With hindsight, I realize we should have hauled the boat out and left it on its trailer. With the infamous boat plug removed, the bilge water would have simply drained out. Now, if the rains don't let up soon, the engine will be soaked once again. Which could mean another long stint in repair at the boatyard.

Like an angel of mercy, Fredo pulls up to our driveway in the Travelall. He hops out of the rig, shirtless and wearing a black bikini bottom as spare as a jock strap. I'm amazed that he made it here.

"Four-wheel drive, man," says Fredo. "This baby is like a tank. Whoosh whoosh. Right through the water. Nothing can stop it."

He's brought canned milk and baby food for Brett, and India beer and plantain chips for us. "You should see all the cars stuck out there—maybe thousands of them. The people eat and drink and sleep right in their cars. They say some people are . . ." he pumps his fist ". . . in them."

I express my concerns about the *Maroho*. "We probably should have hauled her out."

"So let's do it, man."

"I don't think so, Fredo."

"*Capitán*. We can do it. We have an amphibious tank."

Rain is pouring down at an astonishing rate—almost an inch an hour, according to what we've just heard on the radio. We back the Travelall into the street. The water's halfway up the wheels.

"You two are *locos. Locos!*" shouts Sonia.

There are two routes to the Cangrejos Yacht Club. One way goes east around the San José lagoon, through the backstreets of the Carolina subdivisions, while the other goes north through the *barrios,* across the Martín Peña Canal and over the hills of Monte Flores to the coast road. We decide on the latter route. It's longer, but it's over higher ground.

We plow through the streets of Los Maestros, sending arcs of water off to the sides. Rain beats against the windshield so heavily that the wipers are useless. The great trees that line the streets are bent and bowed from the downpour. Soon we reach Manuel Pérez, a public housing project. With water flooding its streets and alleys, it's like Venice but without the charm. Instead there are stark Stalinist-style tenement buildings, made even drearier by the absence of colorful laundry; it's all been taken in because of the rain. Men and women sit quietly on their little balconies, gazing out at the children paddling about in tire tubes.

And then I see the Boy on the Horse. The boy is about eleven or twelve—lean, sinewy, with an angelic face that seems to belie a fierce determination. Oblivious to the rains, he's riding his mangy pinto through pools of water, working the horse as if preparing it for some equestrian show. I have often seen him riding in front of my house, where there's little traffic. The pony must have some Paso Fino in him for despite its sorry appearance—scraggy mane, bones sticking out—it has mastered the gait: four crisp, even steps delivered in an elegant stance.

It's an incongruous sight, this Puerto Rican Huck Finn drilling this sorriest of nags in the pouring rain. The boy is a stern taskmaster, and he lashes the horse's flanks with his makeshift riding crop, a bamboo shoot.

"*Anda anda!*" he shouts. The Paso Fino horse is noted for its *brio*, its pride, with its upright carriage and haughty demeanor—evident here in both the horse and the boy. Once when he saw me watching him from my veranda, he glared back: *You looking at me?* Then he galloped off, as if my very gaze was an intrusion on a secret dream.

There is something about the Boy on the Horse that reminds me of my brother Garrett. Every family has its challenges, and my own has had its share. We were tenants on a perpetually fallow potato farm in New York's Hudson Valley. My father was a failure as an artist but a success as an alcoholic and breeding bull. His growing Irish-Catholic brood essentially raised themselves. Each of us kids has dealt with the poverty and chaos of our upbringing in his or her own way. Garrett shakes his fist at the world and dares it to challenge him. Brian retreats into the secret gardens of his imagination. Neal laughs and thumbs his nose at it all. Kerry huddles in the embrace of close friends. Young Patrick, separated from his older siblings by many years, attempts to finds solace in the herb. And I, the ocean drifter, the one with the compass in his pocket, am forever running away from home.

The stream that borders the *caserío* is now a raging watercourse, and I worry it might carry away the Travelall. But the rig makes it across the deep stretches, and soon we're wending our way through the narrow, unpaved streets of Barrio Cantera.

"Look!" says Fredo, "The Mitas." Huddled under an awning are a half dozen people dressed all in white. The Mitas are members of an evangelical cult who believe that their founder, an old woman named Juanita García Peraza, is the "Spirit of Life" incarnate. As with any sect, rumors are spread about them.

"They say if you have sex with a Mita you go straight to Heaven," Fredo says hopefully.

Barrio Cantera lines the Martín Peña Canal, a sluiceway of raw sewage that runs from the San José Lagoon to San Juan Bay. Sonia teaches Head Start here. The children, all preschoolers, are simply children: curious, engaging, and occasionally boisterous. It's the parents who are the challenge, and more than once some dope-addled hooker will become enraged when she hears that Sonia has disciplined her child.

"You mess with my child, you messing with me. And you don't want to mess with me, *chica.*"

Every day that Sonia shows up to work is an exercise in raw courage.

The culture of poverty in Puerto Rico was described in Oscar Lewis's best-selling work *La Vida.* The book consists of interviews with members of a single family raised in a slum he calls La Esmeralda, but which is in fact La Perla. It's a densely packed clutch of hovels near San Juan, set on a steep bluff that leads down to the sea. The matriarch of the family, Fernanda, is a prostitute, now living with her sixth "husband." The book follows the lives of the son and daughter who move away to New York City, as well as those of two other daughters who remain in La Esmeralda. One has become a prostitute like her mother. In Lewis's words, his book is "a picture of family disruption, violence, brutality, cheapness of life, lack of love, lack of education, lack of medical facilities."

The book has generated much controversy in Puerto Rico. Still smarting from the depictions of Puerto Ricans in *West Side Story*, many are concerned that Lewis's generalizations about the poor in Puerto Rico could stigmatize a whole people, which seems especially unfair considering how far the islanders have come in such a remarkably short while.

For the first half of the twentieth century, Puerto Rico was known as the "poorhouse of the Caribbean." It was as poor as Haiti, with an illiteracy rate of almost 80 percent and an unemployment rate of 40 percent. The average life expectancy was forty years. Then, in the 1940s, under the leadership of their first elected governor, Luis Muñoz Marín, Puerto Ricans began to pull themselves up by their own bootstraps. The entire economy of the island was overhauled. The idea was to bring in what Puerto Rico didn't have, which was capital, to put to work what it did have, abundant labor. The government set up pilot factories in labor-intensive industries such as shoe and clothing manufacturing. Then they invited US manufacturers down to the island to see how efficiently the factories were run. Generous tax incentives usually sealed the deal. Operation Bootstrap was a stunning success.

Today there are thousands of factories in Puerto Rico making everything from computers to pacemakers to pharmaceuticals. Unlike on other Caribbean islands, manufacturing far outstrips agriculture and tourism. The demand for a skilled and educated workforce has resulted in a literacy rate of 90 percent and the highest percentage of college graduates in Latin America. The middle class, once almost nonexistent, is now the largest in Latin America.

But for Oscar Lewis this has not been enough. And he's right. There is still too much poverty on the island. Lewis quotes a popular Puerto Rican saying: *No se puede tapar el cielo con la mano.* You can't cover up the sky with your hand.

We drive over a little bridge that crosses the Martín Peña Canal, which is lined on both sides with shacks on stilts. The flood waters have now risen as high as the rickety porches. Far up the canal, a skinny white dog is swimming, desperately looking for a place to get out of the water. A boy on a porch holds out a stick for the dog to grab in its mouth. But the dog refuses it, and paddles past another porch, where a man reaches out to get a hold of its tail. No luck either. The dog paddles on.

We follow the road up into a hilly neighborhood of Santurce. It's like paddling upriver through a series of rapids. Suddenly a Volkswagen Bug comes sliding down the street directly toward us. Fredo swerves the Travelall to one side—"*Coñooooo!*"—and the driverless Bug floats past, heading inexorably downhill toward the Martín Peña bridge.

"Man, those Beetles are built good," Fredo says.

The Travelall heads over the crest of Monte Flores then slip-slides down a steep street. The brakes grab hold just before we reach the intersection with Highway 26. The highway is a virtual parking lot, full of cars and trucks headed west toward

San Juan. Fat raindrops bounce off car tops and hoods like dropped pebbles. Engines are off, either to save gas or because the vehicle is stalled. Many people are standing outside their cars in the rain, drinking and socializing. It's like something out of the Jean Luc Godard film *Weekend* except that instead of Frenchmen stuck in the longest traffic jam in cinema and driven to revolution, cannibalism, and murder, you have Puerto Ricans stuck in the longest *tapón* in history and driven to rum, *salsa,* and heated discussions about Roberto Clemente's fielding prowess and *Simplemente María*'s pregnancy and Marisol Malaret's fiancé, a bimbo golf pro at the Berwind Country Club. *Ay, Dios,* she can do better than him!

We turn east, against the traffic and toward the beaches of Isla Verde. The road is relatively clear. No one's going to the beach today. We make it to the aptly named Neptune Street and follow Neptune toward the ocean. We turn east on Isla Verdes Avenue, which runs alongside the beach all the way to Cangrejos.

Then we see that up ahead the waters from Los Corozos Lagoon are flowing across the road. The bank has been breached like a Mississippi levee. The waters have flooded a seaside cemetery; the stone angels and Virgins and Jesuses look like sacred navigation markers in the sea.

The road is flooded for a good quarter of a mile. There's no way around it. We would have to drive right through it.

"*Capitán,* we can do it."

"I don't know, Fredo."

I remember reading somewhere that it takes only two feet of water to carry off a vehicle. "I think it's too deep."

"*Bueno.* Let us see." Fredo hops out of the Travelall and wades in. The water is up to his knees. He continues on until he's almost halfway across; the water is still only up to his knees. Then he turns and holds his arms out as if gesturing to disciples.

"A miracle!" he shouts. "I can walk across the water!"

Slowly, ever so slowly, we drive through the floodwaters. Halfway across comes that celestial sprinkler again. The pounding of rain on the hood is so intense it's frightening. This is crazy. All this risk and effort for what? For a boat? A boat that doesn't even love us in return. Laddieee! Laddieee!

We make it across, then follow the beach road another two miles to the yacht club. Laguna Torrecillas has also overflowed its banks, and the yacht club grounds are a shallow lake. There are no other cars around. Unlike Fredo and me, the boat owners value their lives more than their boats. In fact, most boats are already resting safely on their trailers. Those still in their slips sit low in the water. Many are canted over. A few small boats have sunk. Others, their dock lines having parted, are slowly drifting down the channel. Eventually they'll drift out to sea. But the *Maroho* is still tied securely to the dock, and though she's low in the water, she's afloat.

Now to haul her out. I'm worried that, with the added weight of all the rainwater, the trailer's winch might not be powerful enough to do the job. Then Fredo brings to my attention a more immediate problem.

"*Capitán.* Do you remember where we left the trailer?"

"Yes." The parking spots are marked with numbered stakes. "We're in space number twenty-three."

"*Coño.* That's what I thought."

Space number twenty-three is empty.

"Maybe the maintenance crew moved it to another spot," I say hopefully. We tromp up and down the line of trailers, but the *Maroho*'s is not to be found. The dark reality sets in: someone has stolen it. Stolen the frigging trailer. *Ay, carajo!* Now what?

Already, rainwater has filled the engine bilge, and it's almost up to the distributor. We hook up the cable to the shore power to run the bilge pump. But after a flip of the switch, nothing happens. There is no shore power. We are the shore power.

"We're gonna have to bail her out, Fredo."

"OK. Let's do it."

I go down into the cabin to fetch buckets. There's more than two feet of water sloshing around down here. A pair of buckets are bobbing about as if awaiting us.

Rain pounds our bodies as we bail. We chant a Puerto Rican version of the Volga Boatmen's Song. Instead of "Yo-oh heave ho," we sing, "*Qué jo-dien-da. Qué jo-dien-da.*" What a fuck-errr. What a fuck-errr. For every bucket of water we bail, another bucketful falls from the sky. We are living the myth of Sisyphus.

An hour later, we sit on the dock, utterly spent. There is no less water in the boat than when we started bailing. On the other hand, Fredo points out cheerily, there is no *more* water in the boat than when we started.

"I think we should congratulate ourselves," he says. "We have done well. We should go back to the house and have a nice cold India and maybe smoke a little doobie and then I will go home *y me hago cocolía.*" That is, "make some coconut milk"—jerk off. Sometimes Fredo is a fount of wisdom.

We drive back via the alternate route, clockwise around the lagoon, through the suburbs of Vista Mar and Campo Rico and Las Virtudes. The streets are flooded there too, but there is little traffic and the water is not too deep. We should have gone this way in the first place.

Soon we're sitting on the veranda of my house drinking Indias. I suggest to Fredo that he stay the night rather than drive back home in the rain by himself. He does stay the night. And the next. And the next. There's no letup in the storm. But having Fredo here is a delight. He entertains baby Brett with a repertoire of other-worldly sounds. And over a dinner of rice and beans and Spam, he tells us about his dreams for the future. Fredo longs to visit Israel.

"Israel? Why Israel?"

"To work on one of those farms, *tu sabes.* Where everybody lives for free."

"You want to work on a kibbutz."

"*Sí.* A kibbutz." Fredo describes this fantasy in which he is planting fields alongside golden-haired *sabras* in tight khaki shorts. "I saw the pictures in the National Geographic Magazine. Those chicks are *caliente, hombre.*"

Adaír shows up at the door with an invite for a hearty meal at Doña Rita's. The power has been restored. The island is emerging from a very dark funk, as the storm clouds move on at last. There's only a light sprinkling of rain, and there are patches of blue in the eastern sky. The floodwaters are receding. Still, some thirty-eight inches of rain have fallen. Twenty-nine towns have been flooded. More than five hundred homes have been destroyed. Thirty-five people have drowned. It's been the most devastating weather disaster since Hurricane Ciriaco. Yet despite the tragic losses, there have been countless demonstrations of the "kindness, generosity, and compassion" that Oscar Lewis observed in the *barrio* of La Perla.

The *San Juan Star* trumpets the plucky determination of one woman who refused to leave her flooded neighborhood. FLOODS DON'T BUDGE MARISOL reads the headline. "Standing up to her waist in water," the article says, "the green-eyed brunette" remained behind to stand watch against looters.

"She's been a determined girl ever since I can recall," Aunt Ester told a reporter.

There were many Marisols, many heroes, and many lives were saved. Among them, perhaps, a skinny white dog in Barrio Cantera.

CHAPTER 15
La Chalupa

If I am going to be drowned—if I am going to be drowned—if I am going to be drowned, why, in the name of the seven mad gods who rule the sea, was I allowed to come thus far.
—Stephen Crane, *The Open Boat*

"They stole the boat's trailer?" asks Cruz-Cruz.

"Yes, sir."

"It will take months to replace it."

"I know that."

"*Hijo de puta.* That means we can only move the boat by sea. I was hoping you could move the boat by trailer to Puerto Chico. It's on the east coast, only about seventeen miles to Culebra. But if we have to travel by sea to Puerto Chico, it will take another . . ."

"At six knots, another full day."

"Six knots? That is as fast as the boat can go?"

"Yes, sir. Until we can figure out why we can't get it up on a plane."

He shakes his head. "And the engine. I understand it stalled on you."

"We haven't tried to crank it up since the rains. But I'm having a mechanic look at it later today."

"And the compass. Have you calibrated the compass yet?"

"No sir, not yet. We started to, but then the engine crapped out, and then the floods came and then the trailer got stolen and then—"

"*Ay, Dios mío.*"

I head for the yacht club marina to check on our new mechanic, José. Fredo recommended him, although he doesn't usually work as a mechanic. Fredo doesn't know what José does for a living besides dealing *yerba,* or home-grown pot, but insists that José knows boats; he's been around them all his life. His parents are very wealthy and own a fleet of yachts.

"But has José actually worked on boat engines?" I asked.

"*Capitán,*" Fredo said, "the man is a genius."

"What about inboard/outboards? Has he ever worked on those?"

"A genius. A true genius. He's also rich, so you won't have to pay him."

José is already working on the engine when I show up at the dock. He has the wild hair and intense look of the rock musician Carlos Santana. But instead of music, José channels his passion into mechanics. He takes the *Maroho*'s engine apart like he's undressing a lover. "You must work slowly," he says. "Never rush. Never, never rush."

He fondles the adjustment nut on the carburetor. "This is the engine's clitoris. You must make the clitoris happy. Or she will not respond to you."

José's other love is *la gringa*, a blonde exchange student at UPR who hails from upstate New York. "She does it all," says José dreamily. "She does it *all.*"

He says it will take two or three days to have the inboard/outboard purring happily. That's cutting it close to our departure date. Fredo offers to make runs to the auto supply house, and José agrees this would save him some time. I ask him what I can do to help.

"There are some things that are best done alone," says José as he gently slides a feeler gauge between a spark plug gap. It's time to *echar el canelo*, he says. To "toss in the cinnamon." That is, to have sex.

Despite the inroads of English and Spanglish, the language of Puerto Rico remains Spanish. It might not be the elegant tongue of Castile, but *fuá, nene! nada sale por la culata.* Yo, baby! Nothing comes out of the gun butt. Nothing comes out as planned.

My own attempts at learning Spanish have been frustrated by the Puerto Rican vernacular. Sentences are spoken with the rat-tat-tat delivery of a machine gun. Consonants and syllables are frequently dropped. And creole Spanish is rich in idiomatic expressions. Especially about sex. There are the countless double entendres. An innocent question such as "Where should I put it?" elicits howls of laughter in the office. "I made a tortilla last night" can also mean "I engaged in anal sex last night." "To vote" is also "to shit." "Eggs" can mean "testicles." A "palm leaf," a vagina. A "little bean," a clitoris. A simple error in gender can turn "I'd like some more cinnamon" into "I'd like some more semen." I myself have turned "I'd like to quit my job" (*Me voy a rajar)* into "I'd like to engage in unbridled sex." Puerto Rican Spanish can be a social minefield.

A week has passed and José, working on the engine, lends his voice to the Marvin Gaye song blasting from the boombox: "Ain't nothing like the real thing, baby. Ain't nothing like the reeeeal thing." José's unbridled joy springs from the impending arrival tonight of *la gringa* from the UPR campus in Mayagüez. *La gringa*, the Woman Who Does it All.

"She is ready, man," he tells me as he slowly and tenderly screws in the sparkplugs. "Ready to do it all, *hermano*. To do it *all*." It's time to take her out and give her a real workout. The boat, that is. We also need to finish calibrating the compass, especially important since the depth sounder has now stopped working.

"This boat is a *chalupa!*" shouts Adaír. *Chalupa* can mean either a little dinghy or a crazy person. I've decided to invite my brother-in-law along for the compass check. I think getting out on the water is just the tonic he needs.

As we cast off the lines and head out into the channel, the engine is purring quite contentedly. Perhaps José is a genius after all. Though *purring* is not exactly the right word. *Roaring* is more like it. The engine is still so loud my ear drums are vibrating like timpani. But again: as long as the boat gets us there. For that, I'm increasingly reliant on José. José has promised to accompany us to Culebra. But with *la gringa* coming to town, I worry the little head will tell the big head what to do, and he'll jump ship here in San Juan.

There's just too much at stake now. There has been a major setback for Culebra. Lawyers Copaken and Jones had lobbied hard in the Senate for an amendment to stop the bombing completely. The Senate subcommittee, chaired by Senator Henry "Scoop" Jackson, had recently approved such an amendment. But the provision was killed in the House-Senate conference committee. Once again, the intractable war hawk, Congressman L. Mendel Rivers of South Carolina, won the day. (It was Rivers who once declared that the only person who should be punished for the massacre at My Lai is the pilot who tried to stop the slaughter.) Copaken calls it "a bitter defeat for the people of Puerto Rico." Buoyed by this legislative victory, the Navy is forging ahead with its plans to annex more of Culebra's land and increase the firepower of the target practice. As long as L. Mendel Rivers is in power, it seems, the Navy can do with Culebra what it wants. Unless . . .

Unless there is another way to stop them. If Governor Ferré can convince President Nixon to get the Council of Environmental Quality involved, perhaps the CEQ can order a halt to the bombing. So now it's up to us, the Culebra team, to provide Ferré with the information he needs to present his case: that Culebra's environment is worth saving. The team, in turn, is dependent on the R/V *Maroho*. *La chalupa*, the crazy one.

The boat will be used not only for the marine studies but also to shuttle the scientists around the island as needed. The team, including Francisco Torrejón, will travel to Culebra by small plane. There they will board the boat for a tour of the Culebran islands. Mayor Feliciano himself will serve as our guide. At first I was thrilled that we'd have the mayor aboard, but then a familiar apprehension set in. Call it performance anxiety. Especially after the tachometer joined the fuel gauge, the bilge pump, the depth sounder, and the VHF radio in giving up the ghost. At the very least, we need a compass that works. But now the compass, too, has gone haywire. In a test run, I discover that the deviation table we made a few weeks ago is no longer accurate. There's no reason for this. Everything metal or electronic on the boat—that is, every potential electromagnetic disturbance—is in the exact same position it was in weeks ago. Nothing has changed. Unless the magnetic pole has suddenly moved thousands of miles across the Arctic in a geophysical phenomenon not seen in millions of years.

Adaír is at the helm maintaining a steady course, and Fredo is up on the bow, ready to alert us when we cross the bearing line between the tower and the beacon. And yes, we are recalculating the compass deviation.

"*Marca!*" shouts Fredo. We're on the line.

I take a compass bearing on the beacon and jot it down.

At least the engine seems to be running well. The boat still can't get up on a plane, but that would be too much to hope for. We'll just have to plow along at six knots or so. Which is about as fast as the *Niña*, the *Pinta*, and the *Santa María* sailed, and look how far they traveled. And did Columbus ever complain? He would scoff at our concerns.

But Cruz-Cruz does not. It's our last meeting before we set out for Culebra, and he desperately wants assurances that the *Maroho* will be there.

"She will be there," I offer with false bravado.

"No sign of the trailer?"

"Nope. Gone with the wind."

"And the bilge pump?"

"It's still down, but we do have extra buckets."

"Buckets," he says, shaking his head. "I understand the radio is not working either."

"José is rewiring the antenna. He thinks it's simply a break inside the cable."

"And the fuel gauge?"

"We'll just have to top off the tank before we leave. We'll have plenty of fuel to get us there, especially if we're only running at six knots."

"Still only six knots. At how many rpm?"

"Actually, we don't know anymore. Since the, uh, since the tachometer has stopped working also."

I can tell by the pained expression on his face that I'm not doing a very good job of allaying his concerns.

"We'll be traveling close to shore," I add. "And mostly in sight of land. So we should be fine."

"*Cañiña de mono,*" he mutters. Monkey shit.

The night before we set sail for Culebra, the *amigos* throw me a bon voyage party at Pepe's Place. I'm treated to all the drink I want, though tonight I'll stick to Malta India, a dark nonalcoholic brew that is sweet and smooth as molasses.

For good luck, I play "My Sweet Lord" on the juke box. Pepe hates the Beatles because, he says, they look like *mariposas*—butterflies, girly men—especially Paul, "the way he yiggle his head from side to side and the way he look at you. *Mariposa!*" But tonight the choice of music is all mine.

Ramón asks me countless questions about the trip to Culebra. How long will it take to get there? What will you do for food? Where will you sleep? Do you think they have television? It's as if I'm sailing off—like Gulliver—to the flying island of Laputa. I'm surprised to learn that no one here in Pepe's Place has ever actually been to Culebra. But then, what reason would they have had for going there? The need for lab rats? Still, though Culebra might be a distant island and Culebrans distant cousins, they are family nonetheless.

"When you see the mayor," says Wilfredo with the dog named Puppy, "you give him *felicidades y saludos*"—good luck and good health—"from all of his friends . . . here in Pepe's Place."

"*Exacto!*" says Blanquita. There are cheers all around.

Adaír joins me on the walk home. He tells me how much he enjoyed being out on the boat. *Que chalupa!* he says.

We arrive at the gate to my house on Calle Gutiérrez.

"*Capitán*," he says. "Good luck in Culebra."

He thrusts a fist skyward: "And give the Navy the ass!"

Fredo and I arrive at the dock before the last star has faded in the crepuscular light. We load our gear onto the deck of the boat. I look at my watch. José is overdue.

"I was afraid this would happen," I say.

"Maybe *la gringa* is just heating up the sausage a little," says Fredo as he carries an ice chest of food and drink into the darkened cabin below. On his way back up he announces, "He's here."

"José?"

"*Sí.* José is here. He is just waking up."

"He slept on the boat?"

"I think so. Maybe something happened with *la gringa.*" Fredo whispers, "He looks very unhappy."

He also looks very stoned as he slowly emerges from the cabin. "She did it all," he says, shaking his head. "She did it all." He then slinks back down below. Yes, she did it all, it seems, and then she dumped him.

"He took some medications," says Fredo, "to ease *el sufrir.*" *Medications.* Christ. We need José. But not a heartbroken, drug-addled José.

As the *Maroho* sets out to sea, the vial of sacred amulets dangles from the boat's antenna. Doll's eye, sprig of parsley, hair of a white goat, paint flecks from a statue of the Virgin Mary.

We cut through the brown waters off Loíza where two ebony-skinned fishermen give us a gesture of blessing for a safe voyage. *Gracias,* fishers. We need all the luck we can get.

Soon, off the starboard bow, we see the brooding hulk of El Yunque rising more than a thousand feet above sea level. Wispy bands of clouds swirl around the mountain like the veils of a Turkish dancer.

"Hey, *Capitán*," Fredo says with an impish grin, "do you remember Las Pailas?"

Las Pailas. How could I ever forget? "No," I say, "I do not remember Las Pailas, Fredo."

"Liar!"

A few months ago, Cruz-Cruz asked us to scout the boat ramp facilities on the eastern side of the island. We took Highway 3, also known as 65th Infantry Avenue for the Puerto Rican regiment that performed so heroically during the Korean War. And fittingly, we fought fierce traffic all the way to Fajardo. Much of the road is lined with tire and muffler shops, minimalls, and ticky-tacky subdivisions, which add to the tedium of the drive. By the time we made it to the marina in Puerto Chico, we were already battle weary. We took a cursory look at the boat ramp. It was paved and it led down into the water—yes, this will do—then immediately headed back to San Juan. Back into the traffic.

After sitting for an hour behind a truck farting unspeakably foul fumes, Fredo pounded the dashboard and shouted "*Basta!*" Enough! "*Capitán.* I think we have to get off this *pendeja* of a road."

"Fredo," I said. "Go for it."

We turned off the highway onto a narrow road that led up toward El Yunque and into the rainforest. The road climbed higher and higher through towering green mansions and past stunning waterfalls, and soon we were on a winding gravel road that overlooked a bottomless canyon.

Suddenly Fredo pulled the rig off to the side of the road. "*Mira!*" he said, pointing toward a wall of foliage. "See that? That's it! That's the trail. The trail to Las Pailas. Let's do it!"

I could see no trail, nor even the slightest break in the solid wall of green. Besides, it was getting late.

"I don't know, Fredo," I said. "It's after four."

"*Capitán,* you will love Las Pailas.

"We really should get back to the office."

"Trust me. Paradise. Paradise is right up that trail."

We trekked along a dense, narrow path that only a Taíno Indian could follow. There was an eerie silence. Nothing stirred—not a bird, not a butterfly, not even a lizard. The air was thick as rice pudding. Continuing on, we heard the low hush of rushing waters. As we walked, it became a rumble, then a roar, then a thunderous roar as we approached Las Pailas, the pools. And there they were: stunning cascades that tumbled down from the heavens into a series of water-filled bowls. Over centuries, perhaps, the water has carved serpentine chutes into massive walls of rock. We stood before one of the chutes. Slick with moss, it curved this way and that, like a children's waterslide, before channeling the water over a ledge and down a good twenty feet into a churning pool, sending rainbow-hued spray skyward.

"*Capitán.* Un doobie-cito?" He was already rolling a thin joint. I hadn't smoked dope since the baby was born. "It is for places like this that marijuana was invented, *verdad?*" he says. Hard to argue with that. So I took a toke, sat myself down on a boulder, and savored the stunning view, the scent of wild jasmine, the cool spray from the rushing waters. Paradise.

"OK, man. Time to chute Las Pailas." He stripped off his clothes and waded up to his knees in the water chute. "*Capitán.* Come on! You just sit in the stream and let it take you for a ride. Watch me!"

He eased himself down in the stone chute, the water rushing over him and pressing hard against his back. "You put one hand on each side of the chute!" he shouted. "And then you—*adióooos!*" And he was off!

I watched him disappear around one curve, then reappear around another, his hands pressed against the walls, and he was shrieking like a kid on an amusement park ride. And then he shot over the ledge and plunged down into the pool below. His head popped up from the churning waters and he was laughing.

"*Chévere* man! *Qué chévere!*" Really great! He waved for me to follow. "*Venga! Capitán!*"

OK, why not? I enjoy a waterslide as well as the next kid. I kicked off my shoes, took off my clothes, and walked gingerly to the edge of the stone chute. Stuck a toe in: the water was very cold. Then I stepped into the chute and could feel the thin layer of moss that made it slippery. I almost lost my balance— maybe it was the dope—but caught myself before I fell.

Then, ever so slowly, I squatted down in the chute. The flow of water was much stronger than I'd anticipated, and before my butt touched stone—*whoosh*—I was off like a torpedo, shooting feetfirst down the narrow chute. I pressed my hands against the slick walls to stay centered, but at the very first curve, my head slammed against the stone wall. Then, on the next curve, I slammed my head again—*whack!*—and again—*whack!*—on the next curve and again—*whack!*—on the next. Then I shot out over the ledge like a human log. And it was feet-first the long way down into the pool. For a long moment, my body was churning underwater like a pair of long johns in a washing machine.

When I surfaced at last—choking, sputtering, swearing—my head felt like it had been clobbered with a sledge hammer. Blood was now running down my face. The first thing that came into focus was Fredo's smiling face.

"Wasn't that great, man? *Qué chévere.*"

"Fredo, are you crazy? I'm bleeding!"

"Uh-oh. It looks like you hit your head. Maybe you didn't push hard enough against the sides of the chute. You see, you have to push really hard. Some people don't. And some people have died here."

"Died! Some people have died here?"

"*Sí.* Some people. They bang their head against the rock. The skull breaks. Brains splatter against the wall."

"Fredo, you *are* crazy."

I tried to stand but felt woozy. "Oh, shit. I think I'm gonna pass out."

"Oh, don't do that. We have to climb back up."

"Climb back up?!"

"*Sí.* It is the only way."

The walls that surround Las Pailas are sheer vertical drops. There is no path upward except up the falls itself.

"It's OK," said Fredo as he stepped up on the first stony foothold. "It's like walking up the stairs. Everybody does it. It's easy." Not so easy when you're half-stoned, your head is throbbing in pain, and you feel as if you're about to pass out at any moment.

Imagine you are naked—yes, just like in a bad dream—and climbing up a sheer rock wall that's as slippery as soap. Every crack and crevice and outcrop, every handhold and foothold is covered with a sheen of slimy moss. Yet somehow you manage to make it halfway up. Then suddenly a foot slips, and you dig your fingers harder into the moss, but you just can't get a grip on it. And now you're leaning backwards. Heart pounding, you dare not glance down at the jagged rocks and massive boulders below. You try to scream, but nothing comes out. That is my memory of Las Pailas. I have blocked the memory of how I actually made it to the top of the falls.

The next morning, when Fredo and I met with Cruz-Cruz to discuss our scout, my head was as big and orange as a pumpkin.

"What the hell happened by to you?" he asked. I couldn't tell him the truth, of course, but before I could invent my own story, Fredo piped up with one of his own.

"It was the hood of the Travelall. It fell—*fwop!*—right on his head."

"The hood of the Travelall fell on your head," Cruz-Cruz said.

"Well, the Travelall had stalled on us," I said, "and . . . and I had to check the engine and—"

"And it was really windy," added Fredo. "*Coño.* The wind was blowing like *una puta gorda.*" Blowing like a fat whore.

"Yes sir, it was really windy," I said.

"So the wind blew the hood down on your head," said Cruz-Cruz, still trying to visualize it.

"*Coño,* these things happen," said Fredo.

"*Sí,*" said Cruz-Cruz. "I am sure these things happen."

We've come a long way from Las Pailas, Fredo and I. And, despite all the ensuing follies, there is no one I'd rather be making this journey with. As Quixote said to his Sancho Panza, "Mad I am and mad I must be."

Luquillo Bay is now on our beam, and east of the bay lies a quiet cove called Seven Seas. It is protected from the ocean swells by long bands of fringing reefs. I remember snorkeling here with Fredo on another one of our "scouts." The reefs, seldom visited, are surprisingly healthy.

But what I see beyond Seven Seas is disturbing. A sea of white horses galloping toward us. White caps from winds whipping around the northeast corner of the island. The wind is from the southeast and we are still in the lee of the Luquillo mountains, but once we pass them it will be blowing like stink. Now the engine is sputtering. What could it be? Dirt in the carb? A faulty plug? Then it smoothes out once again.

Above Seven Seas are the rugged bluffs of Las Cabezas de San Juan, and on the highest bluff stands the old lighthouse. It was here, in 1898, that American marines from the SS *Puritan* landed. They had been told they were the vanguard of the full invasion force. But unbeknownst to them, the invasion actually took place on the other side of the island. (It was a mishap the US military didn't learn about until they read it in the morning papers.) Thus a small contingent of marines led by Captain Barclay made their way to the lighthouse to await reinforcements that would never arrive.

Word of the Yankee invasion quickly reached the good citizens of Fajardo. A certain Dr. Calzado rode to San Juan and alerted the Spanish authorities. He begged them to send troops to protect the city. But for reasons lost to history, the Spaniards refused. So the good doctor returned to Fajardo and went up to the lighthouse and asked the *American* troops to protect the city. The *gringos* were only too happy to oblige. With Dr. Calzado leading the way, Captain Barclay and his contingent of marines marched into Fajardo, where they were greeted as liberators.

Then word reached Fajardo that the Spanish authorities had decided to defend the city after all. Some two hundred regulars were on the way. Both US marines and Fajardo citizens retreated to the lighthouse to await the attack. As the Spanish army approached, gunfire from the American warships formed a protective ring around the lighthouse, though many an errant shell struck the lighthouse walls, where the damage can still be seen today. But the marines, far outnumbered, deemed it prudent to retreat. They rowed back out to their ship, hoisted anchor, and sailed away. Left to their own fate, the citizens of Fajardo greeted the Spanish soldiers as liberators. It was that kind of war.

When the wind blows from the northeast, it has a fetch of thousands of miles, which generates big swells and heavy seas. The safest route to Culebra is south of a chain of islands: Las Cucarachas, Los Ratones, Los Lobos, El Diablo—the cockroaches, the mice, the wolves, and the devil. The names do not inspire a sense of security. But if the wind is blowing from the southeast, there is no safe route.

And that is the wind we now face as we round the Cape. There are whitecaps everywhere, the crests exploding into long streaks of spindrift. It must be blowing twenty-five to thirty knots. Force Seven on the Beaufort scale. A near gale. If the engine fails us here, only a half mile off the bluff, we could be in trouble.

And that's just what it does. The engine sputters, smoothes out. Sputters, smoothes out. Sputters, then dies.

"Fredo, wake up José! We need him up here now!"

Fredo goes down below and is back up in an instant.

"He just moans and moans."

"Fredo, drag his sorry ass up here!"

I turn the starter. The engine cranks but fails to turn over. We've lost headway and are rocking heavily in steep swells. Then *whooop!*—the wind picks up a boat cushion, and it flies through the air toward the line of breakers. The cushion lands in the pounding surf. Then it's tossed by a wave against the rocky shore. That could be our fate as well. The wind is pushing us directly toward the breakers.

I need to get the anchor down as quickly as possible. But the channel is deep right up to the reef line. With a wind this strong, we'll need to pay out a lot of line for the hook to hold. I'll have to tie on the mooring lines as well.

Big waves wash over the foredeck as I stagger toward the bow with coils of lines on my shoulder. I make it to the anchor chocks, free the Danforth, and ease it over the side. Ten feet of chain rattle through the chock, followed by forty fathoms of braided nylon line. The anchor goes down, down, down. When it's all paid out, I cleat off the line and attach a mooring line to the bitter end. Then pay out another thirty feet or so. In this manner, I attach all the mooring lines until I've let out a good three hundred feet of anchor rode. I grab hold of the line, and I can feel the anchor scuttling along the sea bed. Then the vibrations cease and the line grows taut. The flukes have dug in. But will the anchor hold?

And here is José at last, slowly coming up the cabin steps as if bearing a heavy cross.

"José! Can you do something with the engine?"

He looks at me with the watery, bulbous eyes of the saint in El Greco's somber painting, "The Penitent St. Peter."

"José! Get it together, man. The engine's crapped out and we're about to end up—there!" I point to the breakers.

Somehow this cuts through the fog of despair. José nods slowly. "*Sí, Capitán*. The engine, she needs me." Lurching this way and that, he makes his way toward the stern, pulls back the engine cover, gets down on his knees, and places a loving hand on the warm engine block. "She needs me."

I break out the sextant and measure the vertical angle between the lighthouse tower and the shoreline. Should the angle increase I'll know that we're setting closer to shore and the anchor is dragging.

"*Capitán!*" says José. "Turn the starter *por favor!*" I press the starter button; the engine kicks over, sputters a few moments, then quits again. José removes and inspects the air filter, then does the same with the fuel filter. He removes a sparkplug, smells it, licks it. Then screws it back in.

The wind is gusting maybe forty knots. There's no way the anchor can hold, in this. And it doesn't. I don't even need to take another sextant angle to see that the bluffs of Las Cabezas are getting closer. As are the thundering breakers.

"Fredo! José! Put on lifejackets!"

José goes down into the cabin, then comes back up not with a lifejacket but with a bottle of rum in hand. It's *cañita*, "white lightning." He pulls the cork with his teeth and takes a healthy swig.

"Medicine," he says. Then he unscrews the metal cap to the fuel tank and pours the *cañita* down the pipe. He saves one last swig for himself, downs it, tosses the bottle over the side.

"*Capitán*," says José. "Start the engine."

The *Maroho* sits snugly at a dock in Puerto Chico. A sliver of moon is peeking up over the horizon. The Seven Mad Gods of the Sea have spared us. For now. The problem, José has determined, is water in the fuel tank. It could be from bad fuel or simply condensation. When he poured the *cañita* into the tank, the alcohol bonded with the water, in essence "drying it out." But this is only a temporary solution. The tank needs to be pumped out and cleaned—something we have no time to do if we're ever going to make our rendezvous with the Culebra team. The best we can do is top off the tank here at the marina and again when we reach Culebra. Gas is lighter than water; a full tank keeps the water close to the bottom of the tank and out of harm's way. Unless the seas kick up. Then gas and water are stirred together, and all bets are off.

We carry the cooler onto the dock and take out cold fried chicken and fried bread, but none of us has much of an appetite. Instead, we simply gaze out at the boats in the marina, the rows of runabouts, launches, speedboats, trawlers, catamarans, sloops, fishing boats, and fancy yachts, most of which presumably run. José has descended into depression again, and even Fredo seems dispirited.

Out in the channel, fish-eating bats the size of crows swoop down and snatch up baitfish. Clouds of mosquitoes swirl around us. A zenaida dove *cu-cu-ru-cu-rus* to us, the three pigeons on the dock.

"Perhaps," says José at last, "we should go into town and buy some more *cañita.*"

Medicina. Por el sufrir.

CHAPTER 16

Prospero's Isle

So we beat on, boats against the current, borne back ceaselessly into the past.
　　　　　　—F. Scott Fitzgerald, *The Great Gatsby*

The predawn sky is the palest rose, and Venus, just east of Cetus the whale, is a dazzling beacon. Leaving behind the flashing red light of Puerto Chico buoy, the *Maroho* enters the Vieques Passage. The sea is blessedly still. Fredo, up on the bow, looks happy again, like a hound dog in a pickup truck. José is curled up on boat cushions on deck, out like a light. He slept with the engine last night.

Just up ahead is Isla Palominos, low as a Bahamian isle, with tassels of casuarinas and palms. Three centuries ago the Swedish ship *Katt*, bringing settlers bound for Delaware, ran aground here. They licked dew from the rocks to survive. We give Palominos wide berth as we pass to the north and sail east

189

along the twelve-mile line of reefs and cays. We should be in Culebra by nine o'clock, well before the research team arrives.

José stirs awake, sits up, and takes in the surroundings. It is a lovely morning at sea. But then, remembering perhaps that he faces another day without *la gringa*, he places his head in his hands, lets out a little moan, and lies back down. I'm going to have to do something about José before the team comes aboard. Maybe hide him down in the cabin like some idiot uncle tucked away in the cellar.

Soon we're passing Cayo Lobito, then Cayo Lobo. *Lobo*, short for *lobo del mar* or sea wolf, refers to the tropical seals that once prowled these waters before being hunted to extinction for their pelts. Just beyond Lobo, El Mono—the monkey—comes into view. And then Las Hermanas, the sisters: Cayo Ratón, Cayo del Agua, and Cayo Yerba, "Grass Key," where Fredo says he hopes to retire some day.

Dead ahead is Luis Peña, the second largest of the Culebran islands. Unlike the sparsely vegetated cays we've just passed, it has extensive stands of subtropical forest. Luis Peña looks like an enormous sea turtle swimming south, its shell some 476 feet tall, its head craning out, searching perhaps for an island that is not under bombardment. Once home to Culebra's leper colony, the island is now a prime target area for the US Navy—and off-limits to us.

"*Mira!*" shouts Fredo, pointing skyward, and there high up in the sky are a half dozen Navy fighter jets in formation, their contrails like white chalk lines on blue. The planes climb higher and higher then, at the apogee, they dive back down toward earth, the formation splitting apart like an exploding bottle rocket. One of the jets levels out just over the Luis Peña Passage, flying at a hundred feet above the water. And it's heading directly toward us like a kamikaze plane intent on sinking the *Maroho* for the Emperor.

"*Coño!*" says Fredo. Damn it to hell is right. The jet passes directly overhead, its engine noise rattling our bones, its exhaust plume searing our nostrils. Then it climbs back up into the heavens. Was this just a friendly warning? Have we sailed too close to the forbidden zone? Perhaps. For now we hear powerful explosions as other fighter jets fire upon the shores of Luis Peña. Some rockets strike the beach, others hit the water and send geysers bursting up into the air.

And I'm borne back into the past. To light shows over Danang Harbor, seen through an opium haze from the bridge of an ammo ship. And to the terrible beauty of the Great Dragon of War, spewing and venting and raging against Life. Tracers fired by the Americans crisscrossing tracers fired by the Viet Cong. Red smoke trails against green smoke trails. Rockets exploding in the air like meteor showers. The hills and valleys dotted with puffs of smoke. The jungle flickering with flashes of mortar fire. The *fa-foom fa-foom* of big guns, the *whump-whump* of artillery and the *screeeee* of tracers and rockets. The mountains trembling.

Ah, but I was so much older then; I'm younger than that now. A quarter mile past Punta Cruz and its whitewashed cliffs, I turn the boat east. Culebra itself is in full view, Mount Resaca rising up some 650 feet from the hilly terrain. Culebra is surprisingly green, the rainy season having just ended. Once it was called Serpent Island because, from far out at sea, sailors thought it looked like a sleeping sea serpent. The serpent is awake now.

Dewey, the only port, is situated on a narrow neck between Bahia Honda, a large, sheltered hurricane hole, and Bahia de Sardinas, where the Fajardo ferry docks. In addition to imposing a strict timetable for entering the harbor, the Navy has limited the approach to a narrow funnel.

As we approach the ferry dock, I see *Bienvenidos a la Isla de Culebra* painted crudely on the pier. Welcome to the island of Culebra. And there's Cruz-Cruz, pacing anxiously. When he sees us approach the dock, he has to look twice—eyes shaded with a hand—to believe it.

"Oh, ye of little faith!" I shout, as Fredo tosses him a bow line.

We sip coffees in the tiny plaza overlooking the bay. There's not much here except a few stone benches and a scraggy mahogany tree. Roosters spar and squawk. Kids kick around a "soccer ball" made of rags. A wiry old man has a baby goat in his lap, and he's bottle-feeding it. Though it's only nine thirty in the morning, the sun is already beating down mercilessly.

In the anemic shade of the mahogany tree, Cruz-Cruz, ever the military man, outlines the Plan of the Day. The team should be arriving by plane at "ten hundred hours." He taps a finger on his clipboard to emphasize the punctuality of the operation. A chartered bus will bring them to the pier by "eleven hundred hours." Tap. We should be prepared to depart by "eleven thirty hours." Tap. He flips through the pages on his clipboard until he's satisfied all points have been covered.

"Do you have any questions?"

"No, sir."

"Do you foresee any problems?"

"Nope."

"*Bueno.* I'm glad you made it."

"So are we."

I don't share with him the story of our near-foundering off the cape. Nor my concern about the water in the fuel tank. Why make him nervous? We'll just make sure to top off the gas tank before the grand tour of the islands. Fortunately, Culebra's only gas station is just along the pier from the ferry dock.

Hilario, the gas station owner, is an easygoing man with a ready smile. He's a little low on gasoline, he says, but we can have all we need. He's been reluctant to make his customary boat trip to the mainland to replenish his supply. Hilario's anxiety springs from something that happened a few months ago. He was returning from Fajardo with two thousand gallons of gasoline. As he rounded the north side of Luis Peña, the boat began to take in water. "It always leaks a little bit," he says, "but this time the sea was just pouring in."

He decided to head for the nearest sheltered bay on Culebra, Bahia Tamarindo. Suddenly, fighter jets appeared out of nowhere and began dropping bombs all around him. He lit emergency flares to alert the fliers overhead, but to no avail. Bombs continued to explode near the boat, so close he was sprayed with water. I can imagine the terror he must have felt, especially since he was aboard a floating fuel depot.

"They just missed me!" he says. "*Gracias a Dios.*"

The team arrives at the dock at the appointed hour. Geologists and mineralogists, agronomists and botanists, engineers and planners. They sport binoculars and canteens and rucksacks. They look like bird-watchers. But I don't see Francisco. It turns out he won't be arriving until later, at "eighteen hundred hours," says Cruz-Cruz. He'll be coming on the Fajardo ferry. He had too much gear for the plane.

There are now so many aboard the *Maroho* that I fear it could capsize like a Filipino ferry. Cassagnol, our team leader, distributes little maps of Culebra. I notice that Cruz Matos, head of the Environmental Quality Board, is holding the map upside down; but then Matos is more politician than scientist. Still, his very presence speaks to the importance of our mission.

"Who is that?" Cruz-Cruz whispers in alarm. I turn to see José on the top step of the cabin, swaying like seaweed in the tide, with bed-hair, bloodshot eyes, breath spewing fumes of rum.

"That's José. Our mechanic. Genius. The man's a genius. We wouldn't be here without him." Like someone who's stumbled into the wrong party, José slinks back down into the cabin.

"Jesus Christ," says Cruz-Cruz.

Except for his shiny blue suit, Mayor Ramón "Monchín" Feliciano might be mistaken for a country priest. He's a small, slight man, exceedingly polite, with an unprepossessing demeanor. I want to shake his hand vigorously and say how much I admire his work, but it would sound so . . . so *Hollywood*. Instead I simply welcome him aboard and tell him I look forward to learning more about the island.

"Let us hope we have enough time," he says. "There is so much to see." I find that hard to believe. Culebra is only seven miles long. One town, one school, one church. Seven hundred twenty-six people. A dozen fishing boats. A few hundred goats and cows. As the Navy officer said, a spit in the ocean.

Fredo casts off the lines, and the *Maroho* cruises down the channel. Mayor Feliciano asks me to steer around the white-washed bluffs of Punta Tampico. He is a soft-spoken man, so I invite him to join me up on the bridge where he can address the team from a vantage point above the engine noise. But when he speaks about his beloved isle, his voice is strong, steady, assured, and it cuts through the incessant roar.

As we continue southeast along the coast, he points out a white sand beach, glittering like ground glass and not a soul on it.

"Playa Linda," says the mayor. "Pretty Beach. Culebra has many beautiful beaches that no one is permitted to visit. When the Navy leaves, all the beaches will be open to the people once again. They will be public beaches. No one will own them." *When*—not *if*—the Navy leaves is woven into his every description of the island's future. And what a future he envisions!

Yes, he wants to encourage tourism. "But very limited. Small guest houses and hotels. Cabins, or tent sites for camping. We don't want the casinos or the night clubs or the big cruise ships. That is for San Juan. We want people to come to enjoy nature. To enjoy the wildlife, beaches, the reefs; to see the colorful fishes." In a word: ecotourism. He's a decade ahead of the times.

"We have many rare birds that breed here. The boobies actually nest in the craters left by the bombs. They must hope that lightning never strikes in the same place twice, *verdad?* And of course we have the nesting turtles: the green turtles, the hawksbills, the loggerheads. They are very rare now. But when the Navy leaves, people can come to see them here."

We round Punta Soldado, where a deserter from the Spanish military once waved his shirt to his departing ship, begging to be taken off the island. We then pass through a narrow gauntlet of reef banks into Ensenada Honda.

Off our port bow is a broad cove called Bahia Fulladosa, site of the original Spanish settlement. The townsfolk were removed by the US Navy right after the conquest and relocated to present day Dewey. The locals refuse to call it Dewey; it is simply "Pueblo," the town. Another cove, Ensenada Honda, is deep and almost two miles long, and surrounded by a protective wall of hills. The Navy plans to move a good portion of the Atlantic Fleet here, making the cove permanently off-limits to all other vessels. The mayor seems undeterred by their plan.

"You see that lagoon there? It has a very deep channel. It will be perfect to harbor our fishing fleet. And you see just there? That big field with all those tall cactus? That is where we will build the village for the fishermen. When the Navy leaves Culebra."

We approach a small island at the head of Ensenada Honda.

"Can you smell the *alhelí?*" And yes, a sweet fragrance fills the air. It's emitted by countless white flowers nestled among the boulders.

"And that is Cayo Pirata," the mayor says. "The pirates used to hide there from the Spanish authorities. That is where we will build our natural history museum. We have found many artifacts from the Indians and from the pirates and from the colonists. Scholars will come from all over the world to study them. They will stay in cabins right on Cayo Pirata. Which we will build when the Navy leaves."

He then indicates a small cove on the eastern shore of Ensenada Honda. "That is where we will put the desalinization plant. As you may know, we have very little water on the island. No lakes, no rivers, no streams, not even a puddle. So we will take our water from the sea. Like the people of Israel. Culebra will be like a new Israel."

Taking in the surrounding hills—steep, stark, stubby—Mayor Feliciano talks about his plans for developing the island's agriculture. The target ranges would be converted to grazing lands for cattle ranchers. They would be small *rancheros*. The farms for growing crops would also be small. They would grow produce for island consumption like plantains, lettuce, and avocados. "Now almost everything must come from the mainland. But in time we can provide for ourselves." Self-sufficient yeomen farmers. It's hard not to be impressed by the Jeffersonian tenor of the mayor's ideas. He is like the gentle idealist Gonzalo in *The Tempest*, who imagines being king of Prospero's isle:

What would I do? . . .
All things in common nature should produce
Without sweat or endeavour: treason, felony,

Sword, pike, knife, gun, or need of any engine,
Would I not have; but nature should bring forth,
Of its own kind, all foison, all abundance,
To feed my innocent people.

On the surrounding islands—Cayo Norte, Luis Peña, and
Culebrita—the mayor would release small herds of free-rang-
ing goats. They do not need much water, he says. "And besides,
they will eat all the miserable thornbush—haha!" He asks me if
I have ever tasted *el fricasé de cabra?* Goat stew.

"Yes, sir," I say. "*Es muy bueno.*"

"*Bueno?*" he says with feigned indignation. "*No, señor. Es
buenísimo! Delicioso!*"

Heading north along the eastern shore, we pass Puerto
Manglar, a narrow bay surrounded by a dense tangle of mangroves.

"We have many mangroves in Culebra. We will make all
of them nature preserves for *langostas,* for the lobsters. We had
many lobsters in Culebra before the bombing. When the Navy
leaves, the lobsters will return. As will *las conchas*, the conchs.

"And there, do you see that beach there?" Feliciano points
to a beach with rose-white sand. "Sometimes when you sit in
the sands, you hear things. Whistles. Whispers." He sees my
smile. "No. This is true. Scientists say this is one of the very
few beaches in the world where you can hear this, this whispering."

Thus, in our brief excursion around the island, the mayor
has transformed an arid mound of cactus, poisonwood, and
thornbush into an Elysian paradise of magic and mystery. If

only our study team can do the same. They've been scribbling notes, asking questions, nodding excitedly. Perhaps they can.

As we continue along the north shore, the mayor points out Monte de Corona, where his family lived until they were evicted by the Navy in 1944.

"We had a view of the sea and of Cayo Norte."

He says there have been stories in the press about how the Navy accidentally bombed his home. But it is not true. What is true, he says, is sad enough: friends and family torn from the land they loved and from each other, when many migrated to the mainland and to the States.

"It was not moral. It was not even legal."

The treaty with Spain, he explains, provided that private property would remain in private hands. "The United States government has violated that treaty. Just like they did with the Indians."

But the Culebrans will never give up their lands again, he says. And when the Navy leaves, all properties will be returned to the families that were evicted. *When the Navy leaves. When the Navy leaves. When the Navy leaves.*

Now, off the northeast corner of the island, we must turn the boat around. This is the Navy's prime target area. Strictly off-limits. It is then that we hear a muffled explosion. And another. And another. *KAH-FWOOOF!*

"It sounds like it's coming from Luis Peña," I say. "We saw fighter jets making bombing runs there this morning."

"It is not Luis Peña," the mayor says with a look of concern. "It is closer. Punta Flamenco perhaps. And it is not the sound of bombing. Or of shelling. I grew up hearing the sounds of explosions. I can tell a rocket from a five-inch shell, a mortar from a grenade. No, I have not heard this sound before." He shakes his head. "*Ay, Dios mío.* What are they doing to us now?"

Back at the dock, the mayor wishes us all good luck in our survey. "There is so much more I wanted to share with you. Perhaps another time. I hope that this has been helpful. We have a saying: *Una gota de agua reboza un vaso.*" A drop of water stirs the glass.

He takes leave of us with handshakes all around, then walks toward the lime-green municipal building, the *Alcaldía*, that overlooks the plaza. He stops to chat with a lottery vendor, with a large black woman selling mangoes, with kids twirling hula hoops, with the old man bottle-feeding his baby goat. There's nothing in his demeanor to suggest a politician; he's simply a neighbor greeting his neighbors.

CHAPTER 17
Triggerfish

The moment is illuminating. I am a creature among creatures.
One link in a complex and unfathomable chain.
—Bill Barich, on the reefs of Culebra

The ferry from Fajardo arrives at dusk, and returning Cule-brans drive their battered cars and pickups down the ferry ramp. Others walk, carrying shopping bags full of groceries and store-bought clothes and household goods purchased on the mainland. And there, walking behind an islander carrying caged pigeons, is Francisco, loaded down with gear.

"*Capitán!*" he shouts with that irrepressible enthusiasm. "Ready to go to work?"

We carry the gear to the *Maroho* and lock it up inside the cabin, though we've been assured that crime is rare on the is-land. We also have a watchdog in the person of José, who'll be spending the night aboard the boat.

The Seafarer's Inn is run by a cranky, full-bearded stub of a man named Druso Daubon. Descended from French settlers, he claims hegemony over the island's cuisine. His culinary rival, Botello, runs the only other inn on the island, the Puerto Rico Hotel. Druso serves us queen triggerfish steamed in garlic, olive oil, and wine.

"In that other place," he says scornfully, "they fry their fish in grease. In grease!"

Meanwhile, the team members staying at the Puerto Rico Hotel are served fresh-caught lobster steamed in garlic, olive oil, and wine.

"You don't want to eat at that other place," says Botello. "Daubon cooks everything in grease. In grease!"

The team meets in the lobby of the Seafarer's Inn, where Cassagnol goes over our assignments. Most will explore the island on foot or in jeeps, taking soil and mineral samples, collecting plants, observing wildlife. Francisco and I will survey the coral reefs on the R/V *Maroho.*

Later, on the boat, we study the nautical chart, "Culebra and its Approaches." There is a surprising amount of detail, especially for a place outside the coastal United States. Every reef, rock, and ledge appears to have been charted. I assume it's because of the naval operations in the area.

The coral reefs are indicated by pale-green areas encompassed by a borderline of jagged teeth. Fringing reefs extend from most of the shoreline of Culebra. There are also barrier reefs, some more than four miles long. Patch reefs are ubiquitous, as well.

"If all these reef systems are healthy," Francisco says, "they would be among the most productive in the Caribbean. Perhaps in the world." Francisco has reef fever.

But there is a problem. On the chart, great swaths of sea and shoreline, including most of the prime reef areas, are red-lined as off-limits. They are labeled with warnings such as DANGER AREA or RESTRICTED AREA or CAUTION UNEXPLODED ORDNANCE or EXPLOSIVES ANCHORAGE. The chart directs mariners to the *Coast Pilot* for details. The devil is in the details:

> Mariners are cautioned against anchoring, dredging, or trawling in this area due to existence of unexploded ordnance.

> Mariners are also cautioned against the presence of floating mines.

> The danger zone is subject to use as a target area for bombing and gunnery practice. No person or surface vessels except those patrolling the area shall enter or remain within the danger area.

> *Under no conditions will swimming, diving, snorkeling, or other water related activities or fishing be permitted in the restricted areas.*

The danger zones extend a quarter mile off most of Culebra's coastline and include all its surrounding islands. For boaters trying to determine if they've drifted into a target area, the

Coast Pilot is not very reassuring: "In some areas, the outer boundaries of the danger zones will not be marked."

To boaters considering ignoring the restrictions, the *Coast Pilot* gives a warning: "These regulations will be enforced by the Commander, US Naval Forces Caribbean. No person or vessel shall remain in the restricted areas at any time unless on official business." To violate these restrictions is a federal offense that could result in a fine or imprisonment for a term of five years.

"We are on official business," says Francisco. "The official business of Puerto Rico. I say we survey all those reefs."

"He is right, man," says Fredo. "We are official, *coño! Oh-fees-ee-AL!*"

"If the Navy does not like it," says José rising from the settee like Lazarus, "they can *tocar mi trompeta.*" They can blow my horn.

Well, yes. And they can also blow us to kingdom come, I say. Accidents do happen. But dead is dead. I'm not sure I want to entrust our lives to a field decision made by some pot-headed gunnery crew. I mean, look what happened to the governor, I remind them.

"Besides, we are not charged with surveying all the reefs of Culebra," I say. "Only those in the areas the Navy intends to annex. And that's where we're going."

"You are the captain," says Francisco, clearly disappointed. "But think it over. It is important that we at least take a look at those reefs. We can go in very quickly. We don't even have to anchor. We'll snorkel. No scuba. Take some photos. Make some notes. And leave just as quickly as we came in."

"This is the *Maroho* you're talking about. This is a boat that does not know quickly. It is a slow . . . lumbering . . . sea turtle. And subject to all kinds of strange fits and spells. If we go into a firing range, and the boat craps out on us . . ."

"Look at those reefs in Flamenco Bay!" he says, tapping the chart. "They must be two miles long. And look at the reefs off Luis Peña! They must be twice that long! How can we say we have surveyed the reefs of Culebra without seeing them? My goodness!" He's swearing up a storm now.

"But *read* the chart!" I say. "They are bombing those areas. There are mines in the waters. There is live ordnance scattered about everywhere. It's a target zone, for chrissakes! Besides, that is not our mission. We have plenty of reefs to look at in the assigned areas. And they're not under fire."

The sun is well above the horizon as we set out in the *Maroho* the following morning. *Capitán Manilo,* Francisco calls me. A *manilo* is a fighting cock that's afraid to enter the ring. The truth is, what we're doing is risky enough. No waters in Culebra are entirely safe. Even Bahia Sardinas, the entrance to Dewey Harbor, has one-thousand-pound bombs, primed to explode, lying on the seabed.

We first explore the reefs at the entrance to Ensenada Honda. With Fredo manning the helm, Francisco and I press dive masks against faces, then roll back into a sea of glass. Almost immediately we're treated to a kaleidoscope of vibrant and colorful life. The reef seems to go on and on—too long to cover in a single dive.

Francisco makes extensive notes after each dive. He records the abundance and variety of soft and hard corals, of fishes and shellfishes, of sponges and algae, of seagrasses and sea urchins. It's all very cursory. A full study would take months, perhaps years, but even this little snapshot will provide an indication of the richness and value of the resource.

We measure water clarity from the boat with a Secchi disk, a flat disk eight inches in diameter that's quartered into alternating black and white quadrants. Clarity is measured by lowering the disc until it just disappears from view. In the North Channel we lower it all the way to the bottom, eighty-five feet down, and never lose sight of it.

With the sun now high overhead, we proceed to Culebrita, a mile-long island just off the east coast off Culebra. It boasts the oldest continuously operating lighthouse in the Caribbean. Built in the 1880s by the Spaniards, it features a tower that looks like a chess rook sitting on a box. The Navy uses the lighthouse as an observation post during strafing exercises by fighter jets. They have not practiced here in a while, Cruz-Cruz has assured me.

We anchor for lunch off Playa Tortuga, dropping the hook amidst gray-green turtle grass. Hundreds of glass minnows burst out of the water. The cove is a bustling nursery. Green turtles paddle around the boat, curious about the unfamiliar visitors. These are their nesting grounds. Roseate terns with fierce black masks and forked tails circle overhead, then plunge down into the bay. They, too, breed on the island. The island itself is arid, hilly, and uninhabited. It has changed little for millennia—except for the pockmarks in the hills, incurred by the strafing.

We eat sandwiches of *salchichón*—blood-red Spanish sausages on thick Cuban bread—courtesy of Monsieur Daubon.

"In that other place," he warned us, "the *salchichónes* are not from Spain. And the bread is not even *cubano.*"

After lunch we wade through the shallows toward the beach. There we come upon a series of bathtub-sized depressions scoured into the coral rock by centuries of wave action. Little crabs scurry away as we step into the pools and ease ourselves down into water that is warm as the tropic sun. Tiny iridescent "cleaner" fishes pick god-knows-what off our bodies. None of us feels like talking. It's siesta time. Time to simply close our eyes and dream of an octopus's garden in the shade.

An hour later we are diving the reef off the south shore of Culebrita. And we might as well be dreaming still. I've never seen anything quite like it, except perhaps in a jungle painting by Rousseau. The sheer density of life is astonishing. Giant purple sea fans sway between pale candelabras of crown corals. A thick forest of staghorns and elkhorns stretches as far as the eye can see, and in these clear waters that is very far indeed. There are enormous mounds of star corals everywhere. And flaming leaves of fire corals.

Swirling among the corals are countless schools of brilliantly colored fishes. Pompano gleaming like newly-minted coins. Indigo-blue clouds of tangs. Flotillas of bar jacks, wolf packs of barracuda. There are groupers and wahoos and jewfish the size of humans. Every square inch of the seabed is teeming with life. Starfish, lobsters, conchs, and sea cucumbers. And vast beds of sponges in all the colors of an impressionist's palette: mauves, lavenders, golds, and pinks. The reef resounds with snapping and crunching and clicking sounds—like a concert by John Cage.

I glance up at Francisco floating near the surface. He's hovering over it all, like an airship over a bustling city, trying to take it all in. He gives me a thumbs up, and I answer with an OK sign, two profoundly inadequate expressions of amazement.

"Oh my gosh!" says Francisco, back on the boat. "That was, that was too much, man. I have never seen a reef like this. *Increíble!*"

He hands his dive mask to Fredo. "Fredo, you have to go in and take a look for yourself. *And José!* You too. Jump in the water. It will do you good."

We remain on the boat while the two of them snorkel the reef. Francisco writes feverishly in his notebook. He glances up and studies me a moment.

"If the coral reefs here are this amazing, you can imagine how the reefs off Luis Peña and Playa Flamenco must be." The forbidden zones.

"Yes," I say, not rising to the bait, "I can imagine how amazing they must be. We'll have to dive them. When the Navy leaves Culebra."

With the sun now dipping low in the sky, we head for the north coast of the island to explore the reefs off the eastern edge of Punta Flamenco. On the other side of the peninsula is Flamenco Bay, the Navy's favorite target. This is as close to a bombing range that we—that is, I—dare to venture.

As we head up the coast, the wind picks up, and it's blowing from the northeast. We cruise in the lee of Cayo Norte for a while, but once we clear the island we rock and roll in big swells. I worry about the water in the fuel tank getting stirred up. The *Capitán Manilo* in me considers turning back. But it's been such a fine day. Perhaps the Seven Mad Gods of the Sea are taking the time off to enjoy it.

By the time we reach the eastern shore of Punta Flamenco the swells have deepened, and as they roll over the reef they expose it. It's too dangerous to snorkel here now. Instead, Francisco will simply take visual note from the boat of the length and breadth of the reef.

As we approach the tip of Punta Flamenco, we can see the tall observation post that replaced the one the Navy accidentally bombed in 1946, killing nine sailors. It's called Big Mary. Then suddenly we hear the sound of explosions coming from the other side of the point. *KAH-FWOOOF!*

"We heard explosions yesterday too," I say. "The mayor said it sounded like nothing he'd heard before. He didn't know what it was."

"Perhaps we should see what they are doing."

"Nope."

"Come on, *Capitán Manilo.* Just one little peek."

"No, I don't think so." I point to a Navy Patrol boat that has just appeared from beyond the point. It's speeding toward us. I turn the wheel hard right, heading the *Maroho* back east from whence we came. Not that we could ever outrun them. We couldn't outrun a jellyfish.

Seeing our retreat, the patrol boat slows, and turns. It heads back toward the point. Like a guard dog patrolling its turf.

CHAPTER 18
Flamenco

Almost anything that you do will be insignificant, but it is very important that you do it.
—Mahatma Ghandi

It is an improbable sight: colorful, glittering objects hanging from ropes strung from the mahogany tree to the lampposts around the plaza. They are fish. Dead fish. Hundreds of dead fish.

It is early evening and Anastasio "Taso" Soto, a lobster fisher, stands on a stone bench addressing the gathering crowd of Culebrans. He shouts in Spanish, "Look at what the Navy is doing now! They are killing our fish! They are destroying our reefs! Someone must be told about this before they kill everything that lives in the sea!"

We find out what's going on from a ponytailed gringo known as El Loco, the crazy one. El Loco moved here from

New York City with his wife and three towheaded kids to set up a business collecting tropical fishes for export. He also grows a little *yerba* on the side. It was El Loco's idea to string up the dead fish in the plaza. "It's theater, man. Street theater. That's how you show the world what those assholes are doing."

What they are doing is blowing up the reefs. Slowly, methodically, the Navy is blowing up the reefs. A team of underwater demolition experts has been flown down from Newport News, Virginia, to detonate live ordnance found in the target areas. El Loco was the first to witness it, having ventured close to the forbidden zone in search of some rare tetras.

"I could see them through the binoculars, man. Maybe half a dozen Navy divers. They were working the reef, just blowing up everything. Whoosh! Chunks of coral flying up in the air. I brought the boat closer in and there were, like, thousands of dead fish floating around. Maybe hundreds of thousands, I don't know. It was a slaughter. A mass slaughter. They're war criminals, man." El Loco quickly returned to Dewey and told Mayor Feliciano about it.

Feliciano immediately knew that the explosions must be the same as we had heard from the boat while sailing off Punta Flamenco. He got on the phone to the governor, the media, and anyone else who might alert the world.

Meanwhile, Taso Soto and other fishers went into the target zone to try to stop the underwater demolition work. There they confronted the Navy ordnance divers, who informed the Culebrans that they had entered the target zone without permission and were putting themselves in danger. The Culebrans told the divers in two languages to go screw themselves. They said they would not leave until the demolitions ceased. The Navy ordnance divers left instead.

El Loco's street theater makes the television news. We watch it on an old black and white TV set up in the plaza. We're with Taso and the other fishers who accompanied him into the target zone, among them a pretty young woman named Josefina. The news story opens with shots of fish strung up in the plaza, intercut with sound bites from El Loco ranting about the Navy's demolition work, calling it a "holocaust for fish."

Cut to a Navy spokesman defending the practice as necessary for the safety of Culebrans. It is dangerous work, he says, getting rid of live ordnance. "And what thanks do we get?" he asks indignantly. "The ordnance team was harassed, cursed, and threatened by local fishermen."

"*Mentiras! Todas mentiras!*" Taso Soto says. Lies. All lies. "Except for the fact that we chased them off," he adds with a chuckle. "*Bueno!* We chased them off good! And if they come back, we will chase them off again. If the Navy wants to get rid of us, they will have to blow us all to heaven."

"The women of Culebra must be brave like the men and make the same sacrifices," Josefina says. "We cannot let them take what is ours."

"They want to destroy our fishing so that we can no longer make a living here," adds an old fisher named Rosano. "They want to make life impossible for us so we will leave Culebra. But we will never leave our island. Never!"

Francisco asks if they have any idea of the extent of the damage to the reefs.

Taso says the water was too silted up from the explosions to see. Perhaps later, when the silt has settled, someone could dive the reefs and find out. "El Loco says he saw these huge explosions. They must have done some real damage."

That night, when the ocean research team meets in the Seafarer's Inn, we learn from Cassagnol that the mayor is seeking a court injunction to stop the demolition work. But the Navy is arguing that the operation is being carried out "in accordance with long-standing procedures used throughout the world." That the method being used is "the least damaging one." And that the destruction to the reefs has been "minimal." And besides, it is all for the safety of the Culebrans as well as the national security of the country.

"It is very strange that the Navy would choose this time to conduct such a controversial operation," Cassagnol says. "They know very well that our research team is here. And they know why we are here and what we are doing. You would think they would be more prudent and wait until we had left the island before destroying more of its resources. Is it foolishness? Or arrogance? I just don't know. It is as if they are saying, 'The Navy will do what it chooses, when it chooses. Your ocean survey does not matter. Your people do not matter.' I have just learned that the Navy has plans for at least ninety more demolitions on the reefs."

It's close to midnight and we're sitting on the pier, Francisco and I, having just left Fredo and José at El Loco's, where all are getting stoned in front of the enormous aquarium in his living room. We left them transfixed by pearly razorfishes popping in and out of the sands.

A quarter moon appears, then disappears behind wispy clouds. Mackerel skies and mares' tails make lofty ships carry low sails. Not a good sign for tomorrow's weather.

"Someone has to go in there and take a look at those reefs," Francisco says. "Someone has to assess the damage from the detonations. And document what they have done. Or the Navy will continue to claim that they are not hurting the environment."

Here it comes, I think to myself. *Francisco wants us to do it. He wants us to go into the number one target zone in Culebra, in the Caribbean, perhaps in the world. And then jump in the water and swim around thousands of corroded shells that could explode at the touch of a fin tip. Does he think I'm crazy?*

I study Francisco for a long moment, while he studies the sea. A big fish, a tarpon perhaps, rises to the surface. It rolls over and over in the gentle wavelets, its silvery scales glistening in the moonlight. Then the great fish disappears below with a loud splash.

"Did you see that?" Francisco exclaims. "*Ay, Dios mío!* It is as big as the one we saw in Playa de Ponce." I guess he will always be that small boy from the *barrio* who thrills at every little wonder of the sea. We have that in common. We are both children of the *barrio* and of the sea.

"OK," I say. "Let's do it."

The Atlantic Fleet Weapons Range divides Culebra and its surrounding keys into an Inner Range and an Outer Range. The Inner Range is for ship-to-shore bombing, air-to-ground

bombing, mortar and rocket firing, and strafing. The Outer
Range is for fleet exercises, including mine laying and torpedo
and missile firing. But the Flamenco Peninsula on the northwest corner is subject to all these modes of attack. Last year
alone, 207 ships shelled both sides of the peninsula day and
night. An estimated 750,000 rounds were fired, including sixteen-inch, eight-inch, six-inch, five-inch, and three-inch shells.
The waters are littered with countless unexploded ordnance that
missed their marks. Some ship-to-shore bombs soared completely over the peninsula, striking the island of Luis Peña miles
away. Others struck the string of coral keys far to the west. And
it was off Flamenco where the governor himself almost took an
errant mortar hit. There's a reason they call it target practice.
But today is Sunday; the Navy doesn't fire on the morning of
the Sabbath—God bless 'em. And the demolition team by all
accounts are cooling their heels, awaiting further instructions.
If we can get in and out of the target area before noon . . .

It's after midnight. Francisco marks the chart where Anastasio said the demolitions are occurring—somewhere along the
western shore of the peninsula, where fringing reefs are prevalent. "Taso says there is a marker on the beach, a stack of live
shells that the Navy divers found on the reef. It should not be
hard to find."

As we set out in the *Maroho,* a sheet of high stratus clouds
creeps across the night sky, blotting out stars constellation by
constellation. Fredo and José are sound asleep below, having
stumbled aboard sometime after midnight. They are in deep
cannabis stupors; they haven't stirred since they hit the sack.

The engine noise drowns out their duet of snores. They have no idea that the voyage is underway.

Soon we are passing by the luminescent bay of Puerto Manglar. A shimmering glow reflects off the waters onto the mangroves. We continue up the Culebrita Channel, past Cabeza de Perro, "Dog's Head," and around Punta Garay into the North Channel. The Whispering Beach is now to port. What is it whispering about us? *Foolish, foolish men in such a foolish-looking boat.*

Fredo emerges from below. Without so much as a "*buenos días*," he staggers to the starboard rail, yanks out his *pinga* and pisses into the wind. It takes him a while to realize he's giving himself a golden shower.

"*Coño!* Wind is always blowing from the wrong side, man."

As we leave the lee of Cayo Norte, the northeast wind picks up a bit to maybe five knots, creating small glassy wavelets. Just up ahead is Punta Flamenco. In the predawn light we can barely make out the watchtower, Big Mary. Let's hope the lookouts are as bleary eyed from their Saturday night revels as Fredo and José are from theirs. As for the Navy patrol boats, we've been told by the fishers that they are seldom seen when there are no firing activities scheduled. Still, like some illicit drug runner, I turn off the navigation lights on the boat.

As we draw closer I train my binoculars on Big Mary. There are no signs of life. It doesn't even look like it's manned. I search the bay and the horizon beyond. No patrol boats. I kick up the throttle a bit and the engine spits and sputters. *Christ, not now!*

But it settles back down into a comfort zone when I throttle back.

The muted light of a cloud-filled dawn illuminates the hills above Flamenco Bay, with their bald knolls of mesquite, their cacti and giant milkweed. Lurking among them perhaps is the giant Culebran lizard, unseen since World War II when the bombing commenced.

Accompanied by a pod of dolphins, we cut across Flamenco Bay, passing well offshore of the broad expanse of reefs along the shoreline. On the northwest tip of the peninsula is Punta Molinas with its prominent ridge. A reef extends a couple of hundred yards from the rocky shore. Every year tens of thousands of sooty terns come to nest here. Now, countless birds swoop down on us in agitation. *Leave us in peace!* they cry. *Leave us in peace!*

The western shore of Punta Flamenco might be the most traumatized stretch of coastline on earth. It is a barren moonscape. Traces of its former life exist in the skeletons of trees, the scorched grasslands, the shattered cacti. Only the poisonous manchineel trees thrive. They grow among a motley array of targets: old truck tires, sign boards, metal drums. Battered army tanks squat among cacti whose green arms have been lopped off. Pummeled military trucks sit in water-filled bomb craters. Shattered wood bull's-eyes are set among decapitated palms. There is barbed wire everywhere.

Yet everywhere, too, is the sweet scent of alhelí. Countless white-petalled flowers bloom among torn and twisted tangles of metal. I think of war protesters putting flowers in the gun barrels of National Guardsmen. There are no human protesters here, so Mother Nature has assumed the role herself, spreading flowers among the rubble.

The water is so clear that even in the pale light of early morning we can make out an incredible number of artillery shells littering the sea bottom. We are now cruising close to shore, searching for the visual marker that Taso told us about, a stack of unexploded ordnance on the beach.

And there they are: five-inch shells neatly stacked in criss-crossed layers, ready to be detonated when the ordnance team returns. Just offshore of this spot, Taso assured us, is where the demolitions occurred. There are countless dead fishes floating all about us. And chunks of larger fish. Gray gulls are feeding upon the flesh.

The coral shelf here is long and narrow and shallow. Shallow is good, since we'll be snorkeling. But on the seaward side, the reef drops straight down about forty feet to a sandy bottom that slopes gently until it levels out at sixty feet. We'll need to anchor well off the reef, which means anchoring in deep water, in a strong current, and on a hard sand bottom. Fredo will have to keep an eye on our position and make sure the anchor's not dragging. Or the *Maroho* will be set upon the reef in no time.

I caution Fredo to keep a constant eye on the anchor as he lowers it, especially as it nears the bottom. Last night we heard the story of Olios Añasco, an old fisher who tossed a lobster pot into the water, only to have it land on something that promptly exploded, sending a geyser of water ten feet high.

Even before the hook is set, Francisco is in the water shouting, "*Capitán!* Let's go! Jump in!" One deep breath and I take a giant step forward into the blue. God knows what's down there.

As we snorkel toward the reef we see a sixteen-inch shell sticking out of a huge mound of brain coral. It's like a scene out of the 1902 film by Georges Méliès, *A Trip to the Moon,* in which a rocket lands right in the eye of the Man in the Moon. Bright yellow butterflyfish are pecking at sea anemones growing on the shell casing.

Francisco points out a cluster of five-inch shells in the sands, knocking about in the swirling subsurface currents. The casings are corroded, crusted with corals, and mottled with algae. He signals with the slow flutter of a hand that we should swim very slowly. He points to his eyes, then his fins, as if to say, watch where you're kicking. I can already hear the ping of metal against metal, which triggers a flashback to my voyage on the SS *Green Wind,* bound for Vietnam with a cargo of booze and bombs. And the sound that resonated throughout the ship: *BONGGGG!* Somewhere on the five-hundred-foot freighter there was a loose bomb in a cargo hold. A loose bomb on a ship carrying two thousand tons of explosive cargo. Day after day we descended into the darkness of the cargo holds in search of it. Sounds carry strangely on a ship, and there were bombs stowed everywhere. We never found the loose one. For the thirty-six days it took to cross the Pacific, the sound haunted us. By the time the cargo was unloaded in DaNang, every jack tar one of us was a muttering lunatic.

Francisco points out small parachutes with their cords entangled in the corals. No doubt they once carried flares for night operations, like those I'd seen over the hills of DaNang. One parachute fills with water and collapses, fills and collapses, like a giant pulsing jellyfish. A curious grouper doesn't know quite what to make of the thing, and the fish alternately approaches it and flees from it.

The reef is a junkyard of military jetsam: huge tires and iron treads, twisted hunks of metal, leaky drums and barrels. There's an oily sheen on the corals and sponges and sea fans.

We then enter a part of the reef where the corals appear to be abundant and healthy. But there are no other signs of life. No fishes, no lobsters, no crabs, no octopi, no squids, no eels, not even a shrimp. We swim through this ghost town and enter a vast wasteland perhaps thirty feet in diameter, the work no doubt of the demolition team. Clouds of pearly silt still swirl about. Living coral branches are scattered about like bones. Stubs of coral rooted to the bottom are smothered with sand. Carcasses of fish, chunks of lobster, shards of conch shells are everywhere. The few fish that have ventured back into this area find slim pickings. It's like Dresden under the sea. If the Navy has its way, this could be the fate of many more reefs around Culebra.

Francisco studies a piece of coral, makes a note on his slate, tosses it aside. In this manner, he slowly picks his way through the rubble. He runs a fiberglass surveyor's tape along the bottom and reads the length. Jots a measurement down on his slate, then signals for us to move on.

If the previous explosion site was Dresden, what we come upon next is Hiroshima. It's a zone of debris and carnage four times the size of the other. This one measures some sixty feet in diameter. I can't help but think there has to be another, less destructive way of clearing a reef of unexploded ordnance. That the Navy's top brass has not considered other options doesn't surprise me. But I'm disappointed in the dive team. I know they are simply following orders, but they too are of the sea. You have to be part fish to become a diver. And they are all veteran divers. They know what lives in the sea, what they are killing and destroying. Have they become so jaded that they no longer give a shit?

In all, we locate six detonation sites, the circles of destruction varying from twenty to sixty feet in diameter. Perhaps six thousand square feet in total area. Centuries of coral growth annihilated in a couple of days.

Back on board the *Maroho,* Francisco kicks off his fins, tosses aside his dive mask. "It is worse than I thought it would be," he says. "Much worse. Where they set off the explosives, the coral substrate is completely destroyed. It will never recover in our lifetime."

I mention the "ghost towns" just beyond the impact area, where the coral appeared intact, but with no signs of life.

"It is most likely from the concussive effect of the explosions," Francisco says. "The shock waves have killed everything within hundreds of feet of the explosions." He shakes his head in disbelief. "We must document as much as we can."

He asks me to fix our position. I decide compass bearings won't do. Horizontal sextant angles are more accurate. What I need are three distinct shoreside markers at least forty-five degrees apart from each other. I see an Army tank that isn't going anywhere and an abandoned watchtower. That's two. Then I

see a tall flagpole. That's three. Good. It's then I notice something flying at its masthead. It is a red warning flag. I glance
down at my watch. It's almost noon on a Sunday in Culebra.
The hour of the wolf, when the bombing begins.

"Warning flag's up, guys! We gotta get outta here!"

I quickly measure the angles and call them out to Francisco. "Tank to tower: fifty-two degrees. Tower to flag pole:
sixty-one degrees."

Fredo hurries up to the bow to haul up the anchor. Then
I flip the starter's toggle switch. The engine turns and turns,
but refuses to come to life. It must be the water in the tank, I
think. We'll need to pour more rum into it to dry out the fuel.
I shout down into the cabin to our comatose mechanic. "José!
We need you! Now!"

He comes out on deck, shielding his eyes from a pale sun,
wondering perhaps what planet this is.

"José, the engine won't start. Must be the water in the tank.
Can you pour some *cañito* into it?"

He blinks once. Twice. But says nothing.

"What?" I ask impatiently. Then it registers. "You drank
it!"

José and Fredo exchange guilty looks.

"The two of you? You drank all the rum!"

"*Capitán,* says Fredo. "The *cañito* was calling to us. Every
night, it was calling, 'Drink me. Drink me.' Every night we
resisted. But the last."

"For chrissakes, Fredo!"

"*Mira, Capitán,*" says José. "I can start the engine. I can. We do not need the *cañito.* What we need is . . ." and he taps his head. Smarts, I think he means. *God help us.*

He goes to the engine and fiddles around with the adjusting screws on the carburetor.

"I think I hear something coming," says Francisco, his eyes searching the skies. I hear it too. The distant drone of fighter jets.

"*Capitán,*" says José. "Can you try the starter please." I press the starter button again. The starter turns and turns and turns. Now the battery is dying.

"Maybe we can put up a flag. Like a white flag," says Fredo. "Show them we surrender."

José strokes his mustache and closes his eyes, and I'm not sure whether he's concentrating or has passed out. After a long moment, his eyes spring open with a flash of inspiration.

"*Capitán,*" he says. "Have you turned on the key?"

The key. The ignition key. Right. The ignition key that was installed on the far side of the bridge dash, a good six feet from the starter toggle. Out of reach and out of sight from the person standing at the helm. Once again I had forgotten to turn it on. I turn the key, press the starter, and the engine kicks over.

"Genius," says Fredo of José. "The man's a genius."

We've got a good twenty-minute run until we're safely out of the target zone. The roar of jets grows louder. As does the roar of the *Maroho.* Our collective body motion urges the boat on, as one urges a tired nag to gallop.

At last we're cruising down the Luis Peña Passage, the target zone in our wake. We hear the rumble of distant thunder. The firing has begun.

"See how easy that was?" Francisco says with intended irony.

"*No problema,* man," chimes in José.

"*Como robando un besito de una gordita,*" says Fredo. Like stealing a kiss from a fat girl.

Francisco jots down his observations while they are still fresh in his mind. Every once in a while he asks me to clarify something.

"I cannot read my own scribbles. In that first impact zone, it looked like the broken pieces were mostly *Acropora palmata.* Elkhorn, *verdad?*"

"I think so, yes." What do I know?

"And the visibility was about five meters?"

"With all the silt in the water, probably. I remember losing sight of you a couple of times."

He taps the pencil, in thought. Then turns back to his notes. Pauses again, glances up. Then notices something in the sky. "Look! Do you see those birds there?"

I see four white birds against a mackerel sky. Long, graceful tails. Brilliant red bills.

"Red-bill tropicbirds," Francisco says. "Very rare. And in Puerto Rico found only on Culebra."

I watch the tropicbirds through binoculars. They're flying toward the target zone.

"To see four of them at once is very unusual," Francisco says.

In ancient Rome, the priestly Augurs used to read the future in the flights of birds, taking into account the types of birds, the direction they were flying, and the quadrant of the sky in which they were observed. Four tropicbirds in the northwest sky. What do they augur for Culebra?

Futile the Winds
to a heart in port —
Done with the compass,
Done with the chart.
    —Emily Dickinson, "Wild Nights'

O ne night in December in our house in Los Maestros, we
are awakened by the sounds of pounding on the door,
raucous laughter, and discordant singing:

Llegó la parranda, llegó el parrandón!
Llegó la parranda, llegó el parrandón!
Abranos la puerta, abran el portón!
Bríndenos licores, comida y calor.

Here comes the party! Open the door! Bring us liquor, food, and good cheer! *Los amigos* from Pepe's Place, sporting the straw hats of *jíbaros,* are on a *parranda,* a moveable feast.

The tradition goes like this: a group of revelers armed with maracas, güiros, cuatros, and guitars pay a surprise visit to a neighbor at night. They sing for food and drink. If the neighbor can't provide enough for all the revelers, he or she must join the group. As the evening proceeds, the crowd grows impossibly large, so that no one, in fact, can provide enough drink for everyone. By the time the sun peeks up in the wee hours of the morning, the *parranda* has become a street party. No one seems to mind. It is Christmas season on the enchanted isle.

Standing in the doorway in my skivvies, I pour rum all around, but—*ay no*—the bottle is empty before all cups are filled. Adaír and Wilfredo and Ramón and Blanquita drag me out into the street by my sleeves. Moments later we're all banging on my neighbor's door and singing: *Si no me dan de beber lloro.* If you don't give me something to drink, I'll cry.

Las fiestas navideñas bring out the very best in Puerto Ricans. All that is "affable, just, and generous," as the poet Manuel Alonzo wrote. During the holidays the extended family includes just about everyone. The season begins in early December, picks up steam with a choral Mass on December 15, continues through Christmas Eve and Christmas Day, and then on through the twelve days of Christmas, leading up to Three Kings Day on January 6.

Until the 1960s Santa Claus did not visit Puerto Rico. It was American television, billboards, and US-style shopping malls that brought him to the island. He arrived in his red fur-lined suit and snow boots, absurdly dressed for the tropics. Today even Christmas trees are shipped down to Puerto Rico. They arrive dehydrated and devoid of needles.

The festivities officially end on January 15 with the *Octavitas* when, tradition holds, families visit those who visited them on Three Kings Day. But the partying doesn't quite end there. The Fiesta of San Sebastian in San Juan is just a few days later, so why break one's stride?

This holiday season, the Culebra team has had little time to party. The governor wants the report by mid-December and the Area of Natural Resources is humming with activity. There are charts and graphs to draw up, tables and lists to compile, scientific papers to write. Coffees are poured, cigarettes smoked, ties loosened, shirt sleeves rolled up as the researchers burn the midnight oil. The spirit of Mayor Feliciano seems everywhere, energizing us all. We are further inspired by his recent victory over the Navy.

The mayor has won an injunction in federal court halting the Navy demolition work on the reefs. And now he has filed for yet another injunction. This one would prohibit the military from using the island itself for target practice. The suit names as defendants Rear Admiral Norvell G. Ward, commander of the Caribbean Sea frontier and commandant of the Tenth Naval District; Melvin Laird, secretary of defense; John Chafee, secretary of the Navy; and, for good measure, Richard M. Nixon, president of the United States. Still, in the face of political realities, it's a quixotic gesture. For now, at least, the best hope for Culebra would be a ruling against the Navy by the Council on Environmental Quality. Our report has taken on an almost burdensome importance.

The office has the ambience of a newsroom about to break a big story, the air abuzz with shared discoveries. Except that instead of hearing things like "She confessed!" or "He took a bribe!" we hear "Endangered hawksbill turtles!" or "Rare blue-faced boobies!"

There is little endemic vegetation on Culebra, writes Dr. Jaime Fuertes, the team botanist, but there are healthy stands of manjack trees that provide the staple food for white-winged and zenaida doves. There are organ pipe and turk's cap and snow cacti. And night-blooming cereus and emerald pepero-mia. There is also a unique "boulder forest," where giant boulders are swathed in orchids and bromeliads, a phenomenon found only on a handful of islands in the world.

The geology, too, is unique, writes Robert Cassagnol. The island is of volcanic origin and surprisingly rich in jade. The geological formations have created deep bays, some of which could serve as sheltered harbors for recreational boaters. And a site called Balcón Beach is one of the very few beaches in the world where the sands whistle or whisper when the wind blows.

Culebra's richest assets may lie in its surrounding waters, notes Francisco Torrejón. The sinuosity of its shorelines provides ideal habitats for countless inshore species of fish. The mangrove estuaries serve as nurseries for abundant fishes and shellfishes. Some of these estuaries feature spectacular displays of bioluminescence. The unusual clarity of Culebra's waters enhances the extremely rich marine environment. Some of the most beautiful and rare reef systems found anywhere on earth lie just off Culebra. But this treasure is threatened by the US Navy's demolitions and target practice. When a reef is destroyed, Francisco writes, it can take centuries to recover.

My own contribution is a series of hand-drawn charts that indicate the locations of the reefs we surveyed and key them to passages in Francisco's text. Our collective effort is driven by the conviction that Culebra *is* worth saving

Never one to succumb to the pressures of a deadline, Fredo invites the McCareys to join his family in a holiday feast. As we pass through the front gate, we're handed drinks of *coquito*, a coconut eggnog laced with rum and nutmeg. José is here, and I see he's found himself a new girlfriend. Ana is a Rubenesque woman with a hearty laugh and a heartier appetite, as indicated by the enormous plateful of food she holds. I can tell by the gleam in José's eye that she does it all, she does it *all.*

Fredo introduces me to his father, a portly man with an aristocratic bearing. "*Capitán,*" he says, shaking my hand warmly. "Thank you for everything."

"You're welcome, sir." I have no idea what he's referring to.

Later, Fredo's mother embraces me and says, "*Gracias por todo, señor. Gracias por todo.*" But thanks for what? I wonder.

"It is for what you have done for Fredo," his brother, Nestor, explains. "He had no direction in life and we were all worried about him. Now, thanks to you, he has a goal. He knows what he wants to do."

"Fredo has been really . . . helpful," I say. "I don't know what I would have done without him. So he wants to work on boats? Get his captain's license or something?"

Fredo's brother looks at me quizzically. "No. He wants nothing to do with boats. He is finished with them."

"Oh."

"He wants to work the soil. To plant things and watch them grow. To have his own nursery business. The family is so happy for him."

"I see. Well, glad I was of help."

Later I take Fredo aside. "So. I hear you're off to be a farmer. I mean that's great, Fredo. Whatever makes you happy."

"*Sí.* I will be quitting the boat. I have always wanted to do something on my own. And you know how much I love to be out in nature. So I have been thinking of making a living from the earth. With my own nursery farm. Working in the outdoors. Just like you on your boat. You have inspired me."

"I'm glad something good has come out of it. I'll really miss you, Fredo."

"And I will miss you too."

"So when is all this happening? When will you be quitting?"

"One year, I think." He says this in all sincerity.

"You're quitting in a *year?*"

"Maybe two years. You cannot rush these things, you know."

"Right. No need to rush into it. *Bueno.* See you at the dock then on Monday."

He gives me a salute. "At your service, *Capitán!*"

A feast has been laid out on tables in the courtyard. There are grilled blood sausages stuffed with rice, cilantro, and garlic. Mounds of rice and pigeon peas. Bowls of chicken stew. Plat-

ters of plantains in their every incarnation. A whole roast pig-
let. The drinking and feasting and music continue until deep
into the night.

The following day, bleary-eyed and hung over, I mark up
the last of the series of charts and turn them over to Francisco.
He studies them a moment. Traces a finger over Playa Flamenco on Chart #3.

"We will get them on this one," he says, referring to the
reefs destroyed by the demolition team. I just wish I could
share his optimism. I can't help thinking all our efforts will be
for naught. That our Culebra report will be like a message in
a bottle tossed into a sea of government bureaucracy, where it
will bob unnoticed until it washes ashore on Delila's desk. The
graveyard of paperwork.

Christmas Day is spent with *la familia* Ríos. Sonia and
Doña Rita are joined by relatives in the making of the *pasteles.*
Pasteles are the most cherished holiday offering. They are a kind
of tamale, filled with spiced pork, chickpeas, raisins, olives, and
chili peppers, set in a paste of yautía, plantains, and milk, then
wrapped in green banana leaves and boiled. *Pasteles* take hours
to make, and the process itself is a communal event for the
women folk, a chance to catch up on family gossip and discuss
the latest tribulations of *Simplemente María.*

The men retreat to the patio to talk politics and sports. The
conversation inevitably turns to the great Roberto Clemente.

"He can throw a runner out from his knees, *coño!*" Adaír
says. "From his *knees!*" Adaír is in fine spirits. Like Fredo, he
too has found a new direction in life. He'll be taking flying les-

sons on the GI Bill. He wants to pilot small planes and spend his life in the skies.

A voice is heard from somewhere singing in Spanish:

Traigo un ramillete
Traigo un ramillete
de un lido rosal,
un año que viene
y otro que se va.
Un año que viene
y otro que se va.

I bring a bouquet
I bring a bouquet
from a rosebush,
One year is coming
And another is going.
One year is coming,
and another is going.

And what a year it has been for Puerto Rico. Yes, it's seen torrential rains, flash floods, an earthquake, student strikes, and the continued bombing of Culebra. But it has also seen miracles. It was the year when one of Puerto Rico's own, Marisol Malaret, an orphan born in *jíbaro* country—can you believe it, *nena?*—was crowned Miss Universe. And the year is not yet over.

On December 28, the Feast Day of the Holy Innocents, Congressman L. Mendel Rivers suddenly drops dead at the age of sixty-five. It's hard to mourn the man. In fact, never has *schadenfreude*, the pleasure derived from the misfortune of another, felt so sweet. With the passing of L. Mendel Rivers, the Navy has lost its most stalwart ally in Congress.

And this only twenty-one days after four red-billed tropic-birds were seen in the northwest skies of Culebra.

CHAPTER 20
Redemption

Audacity, more audacity, always audacity will save the Republic.

—George Jacques Danton

It has been said that a single, small, and seemingly inconsequential action can set into motion events of great significance. The theory was first postulated with a question: "Could the flap of a butterfly's wings in Brazil set off a tornado in Texas?" The passing of L. Mendel Rivers appears to have had such an effect. His body is barely laid to rest when whispers are heard in the halls of Congress of a potential shift in political power. Only a week later, legislation to stop the bombing in Culebra is revived in Congress.

And now the ever-audacious Mayor Feliciano has decided to take Culebra's cause to the United Nations. He will plead his case to the UN Special Committee on Colonialism. An admo-

nition by the UN on the mistreatment of an American "colony" would—if nothing else—be a political embarrassment to
an America that seems to be growing shorter of friends by the
day. As would the global realization that the Land of the Free—
Down with King George!—actually *has* a colony. The US State
Department sounds the alarm. They order the Navy to take
into account "global political ramifications" in their relationship with Culebra because—and this is a direct quote from the
State Department spokesman—"Culebra is, after all, out there
in the middle of the ocean." Whatever.

Emboldened, perhaps, by these events, Governor Ferré
makes his move at last. The governor sends a letter to President Nixon. His request: that the Council for Environmental
Quality serve as the final arbiter in the dispute. He will stake
Culebra's future on the strength of the team's report on the
value of the island's natural resources. For Ferré, the direct appeal to the president means the governor is putting his pride,
prestige, and political future on the line. Nixon is the consum-
mate political animal. He will wet his finger, hold it up to the
wind, and determine which course of action will best serve the
interests of Tricky Dick. He'll soon be up for re-election, and
there have been indications that he's worried the Culebra issue might influence the Catholic vote. On the other hand, he's
been the target of protesters and other "nattering nabobs of
negativism," as his vice president calls them. And Nixon does
have a vengeful streak. But if he spurns the governor's appeal it
will be yet another humiliating blow for Luis A. Ferré, who will
get the ass once again.

La Fortaleza, the Governor's Palace, sits on a high bluff above the ancient gates to the Old City with a stunning view of San Juan Bay. It looks like a Moorish castle, powder blue and trimmed in white. In the inner courtyard is a stopped clock, its hands forever frozen at half past four. It was at this precise moment that the Spanish governor surrendered to the American troops, a moment the governor duly marked with a blow of his sword to the clock.

There are lush gardens on the palace grounds, and a quiet reflecting pool. I envision Governor Ferré, the General in His Labyrinth, pacing anxiously among the stately palms and silk-cotton trees while he awaits word from the most powerful man in the world. When will he have an answer? Today? Tomorrow? Never?

Three Kings Day is celebrated January 6, the Feast of the Epiphany. For centuries it has been traditional in Puerto Rico for the three Magi to bring gifts to the children. The night before, the children leave straw in a shoebox under their beds—food for the camels of the Wise Men. If the children have been good, the Three Kings—Gaspar, Melchior, and Balthazar—will leave them sweets and little gifts.

We set a shoe box full of clipped grass under the bed. Tuck the wee one in. But not long after he has nodded off, there's a loud banging on the front door. Please God, no, I say. Not another *parranda*. Doesn't anyone on this island ever *sleep?* A peek through the window and, yes, it's the Usual Suspects. Adaír and Ramón and Blanquita and Wilfredo. And—*ay no!*—they are singing:

Los tres Santos Reyes, y los sé contar
Los tres Santos Reyes, y los sé contar

But they haven't come to party. They've come to drop off gifts for Brett. A round of *coquitos*, a few warm embraces, and they're gone. *Gracias a Dios.*

As morning light falls on La Fortaleza, softly illuminating the clock that's forever frozen at precisely half past four, the governor opens a letter from the Office of the President of the United States. It reads in part:

> Dear Governor Ferré:
> You have requested that I designate some appropriate agency to participate in this study with such authority from the President that a just and agreeable solution will emerge. By copies of this letter to the Secretary of Defense and the chairman of the Council on Environmental Quality, I am today directing that the Council take part in the study, acting in an advisory capacity. You can be sure that the chairman of the council will be in continuous touch with me on this matter.
>   With warm personal regards.
>   Sincerely,
>   Richard Nixon

The governor's gambit has paid off. Nixon—whatever his motives might be—has acceded to Ferré's request. The CEQ will now play a key role in determining Culebra's fate. It's a clear defeat for the Navy. Already under siege—from the courts, the Congress, the State Department, the UN, and the press—the

Navy must now contend with the damned tree huggers as well. For the first time, the Navy finds itself outgunned, outmanned, and outmaneuvered in the battle for Culebra.

Culebra's lawyer Richard Copaken is quick to seize the opportunity. He presses Navy Secretary Chafee for some sort of compromise agreement. Only a few weeks ago, the Secretary refused even to take Copaken's phone calls. But now he's forced to bargain with the young upstart. What follows is a marathon series of negotiations involving dozens of politicians, five political parties, and two distinct cultures fifteen hundred miles apart. All those deliberations take place during the holiday season, when business-as-usual means no business at all. And yet the result is nothing short of a miracle.

One January morning, I pick up a copy of the *San Juan Star*. The headline jars me fully awake: NAVY TO SLASH CULEBRA ACTIVITY. Must be a misprint. The more I read, the more incredible it seems. On the orders of Navy Secretary Chafee, there will be no annexation of Culebran land. No barring of residents from Culebra's shores. No demolition of its coral reefs. No guided missile target practice. No Walleyes and Bulldogs and Shrikes. The Navy has struck her colors.

It's a stunning reversal of fortune—and surprising, in how quickly it has come about.

"In the end," Copaken is quoted as saying, "we proved that right, truth, and justice can prevail against the mightiest navy in the world."

We celebrate with shots of Palo Viejo at Pepe's Place. I'm permitted once again to play "My Sweet Lord" on the juke box.

"The Navy got the ass, man," Adaír says. "They really got the ass."

"Yes, they did, *hermano*."

"So . . . the *chalupá*," says Wilfredo with the dog named Puppy. "The *chalupa* was worth something after all."

"No. I wouldn't go that far," I say. The *Maroho* was a mere gunboat in the battle to save Culebra. The Navy was defeated by a confluence of disparate forces that just happened to come together at a critical moment. Credit a butterfly—or perhaps even those four tropicbirds seen in the northwest sky of Culebra. The lion's share of the credit belongs to Culebra's tenacious young lawyers, Richard Copaken and Tom Jones, who orchestrated the battle, and the man who inspired them, Mayor Ramón "Monchín" Feliciano.

On a windblown day, the mayor drives a battered municipal sound truck around the dirt roads of Culebra. Through crackling old speakers he announces an important town meeting to be held this evening in the plaza.

At seven o'clock, Anastasio Soto, head of the Fisherman's Association, calls the meeting to order. He steps up onto a weathered stone bench and faces the crowd of fishers, farmers, teachers, and shopkeepers.

"The mayor has some important news for the people of Culebra," he says. "I will let him tell it."

Feliciano then takes Soto's place up on the stone bench. The Navy, he says, has offered to sign a peace treaty with Culebra. It is now up to the people of Culebra to decide if they will accept the terms. He will offer no opinion on the proposal. "It is for you to decide, not for me to decide for you." Whatever his fellow Culebrans choose to do, he will follow their will.

He introduces Tom Jones and Richard Copaken. Standing on the bench, Jones is as tall as Copaken is short. The treaty doesn't go far enough, Jones tells the crowd in fluent Spanish, but it is still worthy of their approval. He assures the Culebrans that both he and Copaken remain committed to fighting for a complete withdrawal by the Navy.

Then Copaken explains the terms of the treaty. "The Navy has agreed to abandon its plans to acquire an additional thirty-two hundred acres of the island."

There are murmurs of approval from the crowd, but others hush them. They want to hear the rest.

"Furthermore," Copaken says, "the entire shoreline of Culebra will be open to the public again."

More murmurs, more hushes.

"Target practice will be restricted only to Punta Flamenco. And even that will end when the Navy has found a suitable alternative."

This last point doesn't quite sit as well. "How long will that take?" someone asks. "Months? Years?"

"I should think three years would be a reasonable time to find an alternative," says the mayor. "We will argue for that. The treaty allows us to continue to fight for a complete withdrawal of the Navy."

The entire treaty is read aloud verbatim, once in English, twice in Spanish. Then Taso Soto announces it is time for a decision. Do the people of Culebra authorize the mayor to sign the treaty with the Navy? He asks those in favor to step to his right, under the mahogany tree. Those opposed he asks to step to his left.

All eyes fall on the mayor. Calmly and deliberately, he steps to the right of Taso Soto. His fellow Culebrans look to each other, then to the modest, self-effacing man who has never wavered in the battle for Culebra.

"I stand with you, Monchín," says a wiry old man as he takes his place at Feliciano's side. Then, slowly but surely, all but a few join the mayor. They all stand together under a mahogany tree in the plaza of a little town called Pueblo.

"*Eso es,*" says Taso Soto. There you have it.

A few days later, the town hall is overflowing with official signatories and witnesses to the treaty. Sen. Rafael Hernandez Colón is there, as is Governor Luis A. Ferré. Representing the US Navy is Secretary John Chafee. He looks disoriented— where is this place anyway? He's joined by the stiff and embittered Admiral Norvell G. Ward, who fought the agreement to the very end.

Without even a modicum of ceremony, Secretary Chafee puts his signature to the document. Then Mayor Feliciano adds his. *Eso es.* When they all step out of the Alcaldía, Culebrans applaud the mayor and pat him on the back. Chafee hurries off with the disgruntled Admiral to an awaiting Navy helicopter.

The governor tarries a while longer, unsure of his welcome here. The islanders have not forgotten his initial reluctance to take up their cause. He walks through the plaza, greeting the woman selling mangoes, the vendor selling lottery tickets, the fisher mending his net, and the old man bottle-feeding his baby goat. He seems surprised, grateful, and even a little hopeful, when each accepts his hand. *Y dónde hay esperanza, hay redención.* And where there is hope, there is redemption.

January 15, the Octavitas, is the official end of the Christmas holiday season in Puerto Rico. We celebrate with an office party. An inducement, perhaps, to lure everyone back to work. Gabo has hung Tibetan prayer flags around the water cooler.

"That is the Wind Horse," he explains. "It brings good energy to all. That is the Snow Lion, for courage. That is the flag of the Thousand Eyes; it returns all gossip and bad intentions back to the sender."

"Can we take that one down?" asks Delila, looking guilty.

Llorlli has brought the cakes and candies. Mercedes, the rum and coconut juice. And Ambrosio has brought a new off-color joke to share:

"Two *jíbaros* go to Nueva York and they see a sign for a vendor selling hot dogs. 'Hot dogs?' says Juan Bobo. 'They eat dogs in America?'

"'If that is what the *gringos* eat,' says José, 'then we should try one to learn their ways.' So they each order a hot dog.

"'*Ay, Dios mío!*' says Juan Bobo, looking at the long thing in the bun. 'Do you see this? What part of the dog did you get?'"

Cruz-Cruz is beaming with the news that he's been appointed to Puerto Rico's Environmental Quality Board. He has other news as well. Our report on the island will not wither away on some shelf as I had presumed would happen. Instead it will find new life, not as an environmental tract to be used against the Navy but as a blueprint for Culebra's future. There has been concern that the withdrawal of the Navy from the island will make Culebra instantly vulnerable to rapacious developers. To prevent this, the Puerto Rico Planning Board is planning to zone the entire island as residential—the most restrictive classification—until a master plan can be drawn up. That master plan will rely heavily on our environmental report for its recommendations.

Any new economic development will face some daunting challenges. The entire island has only fifteen miles of paved road, about fifty telephones, and one small airport runway that is subject to fierce crosswinds. There is little water and barely enough electric power to meet the island's current needs. Yet there is one industry where these limitations can be seen as a blessing rather than a curse. Echoing Mayor Feliciano's suggestions, the team's report envisions Culebra as a center for ecotourism. This is a place that hikers and birders, sailors and scuba divers would consider paradise.

Ecotourism is also an industry that would allow the island to retain its small-town charm. Unlike many political figures who become instant celebrities, the mayor shows no inclination to remain in the limelight. His fifteen minutes of fame appear to have passed and, if anything, he seems relieved. Besides, he has work to do. He is still concerned about the hundreds of Culebrans who were forced into exile by the Navy. "We would like to make Culebra a place where they would like to return and live," he says.

I ask Cruz-Cruz if he'll still be involved in our oceano-graphic survey around the island. It's slated to resume in February.

"*Ah,* the *caca!* How could I ignore the problem of the *caca?* The oceanographic study shall go on, *Capitán.* In fact, we are bringing down two scientists from the Woods Hole Oceano-graphic Institute in Massachusetts to take charge of it. They have many years' experience. They can teach you much. Of course, we will also have Puerto Rican scientists working with them."

He nods toward Francisco, who has just arrived. "Francisco Torrejón will be joining you. He will be in charge of the marine biology component of the study." Music to my ears.

"*Capitán!*" says Francisco with a slap on my back. "I guess after Culebra I can't call you *Capitán Manilo* anymore."

"I'm sure there will be times when you will want to."

"Oh, I'm sure of that too," he says. "Like when we go to Arecibo."

"Arecibo?"

"*Sí.* It is one of the areas we will be studying. They have a lot of pollution in the bay. It is from the *mataderos.* Where they slaughter the pigs, the goats, the cows. All the blood and the guts go—sloosh—right into the water. It is terrible. But the sharks love it. The bay is full of them."

"And? So?"

"So we will have to document this. We will have to dive in the bay. You and me. And the tiger sharks, the bull sharks, the hammerheads, the great whites. Hahaha!" He sees the look on my face. "I am just kidding. There are no great whites."

It is a starry, starry night, and I'm standing at the edge of the sea. The waters are especially calm. There are two moons: a half moon in the sky and its perfect reflection in the sea. I'm not alone. For tonight is the Feast of Saint John the Baptist. Thousands have gathered here on the beaches of San Juan for a communal baptism.

The tradition has to do less with Christian ritual and the cleansing of sins, and more with the ritual's pagan origins. In Greek mythology, initiates seeking advice from an oracle were baptized in the sanctuary of Trophonius. They were ceremoniously bathed, anointed with oils, then offered a drink of the Waters of Forgetfulness. The drink assured that all bad memories would be forgotten. Then they were given a drink from the Waters of Remembrance to retain only the good memories.

As midnight approaches in San Juan, the crowd on the beach begins to form into an impossibly long line, a miracle in itself given Puerto Ricans' love of chaos. Everyone takes the hand of the person on each side of him or her. I look to my right and to my left, and there are friends and family as far as I can see.

At the stroke of twelve, we slowly walk backward into the sea for the traditional three dips—and the promise of spiritual renewal, the cleansing of one's soul, and the transformation of one's life. Because, more than a route to adventure or escape, that is what the sea offers.

That has been its gift to me.

Epilogue

It has been long years since I called Puerto Rico home. We left after the year-long oceanographic survey was completed. Ever the restless spirit, I've found a new calling as a documentary filmmaker, most recently for National Geographic. But I return to the island often, sometimes to work on a film but other times to simply "savor the rice and beans," as the Puerto Ricans say.

Francisco Torrejón has remained a good friend over the years. He works with his sons as an environmental consultant and lives in a stunning home overlooking the sea. We still share the occasional adventure: a night dive in a luminescent bay, snorkeling on a secret reef, beachcombing on a deserted cay. But mostly we sip rum on his veranda and spin tales like two old sea dogs.

We've both lost track of Fredo. He did travel to Israel and live on a kibbutz for a while. And I can see him racing

some battered Sussita down the streets of Old Jerusalem, all
the while tossing *piropos* to the *sabras*. On his return to Puerto
Rico, Fredo started his own nursery business. It supplied flowers and plants to hotels. But the business went belly-up, and
Fredo simply folded his tent and disappeared. I went to his
parents' home once to find out where he'd moved to, but the
gracious mansion had been torn down to make room for yet
another hotel. Years later, I ran into José. He'd heard rumors
that Fredo, now with wife and kids, had moved somewhere
up in the central highlands. It's not hard to imagine Fredo living the life of a *jíbaro*. Swinging in a hammock overlooking a
mountain stream. Savoring the trilling tropical birds, the scent
of gardenias and, of course, a good pipe. And, yes, there would
be countless little Fredos and Fredas scampering around.

Recently I took the ferry to Culebra from Fajardo. The
ferry is full of day-trippers, ecotourists, and scuba divers. The
Culebrans, as always, are distinguished by their bags of groceries and other assorted purchases from the mainland. Though
nowadays they're more likely to be bringing home plasma TVs
than used tires.

It's not much more than two hours by ferry, and it's a lovely
ride. The wind is from the northeast in winter, and we sail
in the lee of the string of cays that lead to Culebra. Las Cucarachas, Los Ratones, Los Lobos, El Diablo. Though wild and
scruffy still, they don't seem as treacherous as they did when we
sailed on the *Maroho*.

On Dewey's public pier, visitors arriving by boat are still
greeted by the hand-painted sign, *Bienvenidos a la Isla de Cule-*

bra. Welcome to the Island of Culebra. And just beyond the pier stands the Seafarer's Inn, where I stayed during our survey so many years ago. It is now called the Hotel Kokomo, after the Beach Boys song I assume, and is under new ownership. The former owner, Druso Daubon, the curmudgeon who served us that fine queen triggerfish steamed in garlic, olive oil, and wine, now runs a B&B in the hills above town. The culinary torch has been passed to his daughter Jennifer, who runs Juanita Bananas, a restaurant featuring dishes with organic and hydroponic ingredients.

Culebra has grown some. There are now more than two thousand residents, about three times as many as when I first visited the island. Still, there are no golf courses, no mega-resorts, no boutiques, no mini-malls, no McDonald's. Drinking water comes from the ancient desalinization plant. And industry studiously avoids the island. The factory for breeding lab rats is long gone. Now, the island's largest employer is Baxter International. They manufacture bladder irrigation kits.

The island has the laid-back ambience of Key West. The sign on a roadside stand called Island Woman seems to say it all:

Closed Some Days. Open Others.

I stop for a drink at a place called Mamacita's. It's an outdoor café on the boat canal that links Dewey Bay to Ensenada Honda. Just in sight is a drawbridge, which the waiter tells me never seems to work. I half expect Hemingway to sidle up to the bar and order a *mojito*. As for me, I settle for a local drink called the "bushwacker," guaranteed to make you want to run with the bulls of Pamplona.

I check in at the Villa Boheme, a very Mediterranean guest house, with its Roman arches and seaside patio. The rooms overlook Ensenada Honda. Once coveted by the Navy as a hurricane hole for warships, the bay is now dotted with sailboats and cruisers at anchor. Villa Boheme is run by a former major-league baseball player named Rico Rossy. Rico had an intermittent career as a utility player with the Atlanta Braves, the Kansas City Royals, and the Seattle Mariners. He collected maybe a season's worth of at-bats in his twelve years in the majors.

"Good field. No hit," he says good-naturedly when I ask him about those years. Rossy played his last major league game a few years ago, then hung up his spikes and came home to Puerto Rico. He's found a new life far from the madding crowds—the baseball crowds, that is—and has become a passionate fan of Culebra.

"There is everything here," he says. "And there is nothing here. Which is why it is so fantastic."

The next day, I pack water and sunblock, mask and snorkel and set out to get reacquainted with the island. But this time I go by land instead of by sea, by scooter instead of by boat. It's a clear day and surprisingly cool with the strong northeast winds of the Culebran winter.

My first stop is the National Wildlife Refuge office. It sits on a gentle hill overlooking Ensenada Bay. Just outside the office is a peppy group of teenagers from Culebra's Youth Conservation Corps. A wildlife biologist named Teresa is distributing short pieces of plastic piping that will be used in today's mission: planting red mangrove seedlings on a denuded stretch of lagoon. Teresa is a gracious woman from South Carolina who's been studying marine life in Culebra for more than a decade.

"With the way federal funding is," she says, "we couldn't do half of what we do without these kids." They clear hiking trails, clean up beaches, raise fences to keep out livestock or to protect turtle nests, build greenhouses, and restore mangroves.

"Oh, and they've become passionate birders," she adds. "Once a year we band a colony of sooty terns on Peninsula Flamenco. It's their chance to visit an area that's off-limits to everyone else."

By 1982, all Navy property on Culebra had been transferred to either the Culebrans or the US Fish and Wildlife Service. All but one lonely Navy observation post on the northern end of the island. The USFWS (that is, their team of two) watches over more than ten thousand acres of wildlife refuge including Mount Resaca, Peninsula Flamenco, and some twenty-two small islands—about a quarter of the Culebran archipelago's total landmass. There can be no development on this land, which means little or no damage from erosion, sedimentation, or pollution. Visitation to most areas is highly restricted. And in those areas where one can visit, a handout brochure warns that it is prohibited to bother, hunt, or possess birds, lizards, snakes, turtles, or crabs; or to collect or possess live or dead corals. Furthermore, all types of "live or dead plants" are protected.

Not long after the Navy relinquished title to Culebra's lands, they shifted target practice to the nearby island of Vieques. And a new battle began, to take back Vieques from the Navy. The struggle went on for some twenty-five years, drawing into the fray environmental advocates such as Ricky Martin, Robert F. Kennedy Jr., and Martin Sheen. Rafael Cruz-Cruz was asked to conduct a study of the impact of the explosive contaminants on the environment. Francisco also contributed to the flurry of environmental tracts. Like our Culebra study, their purpose was to provide ammunition for the Vieques legal team. Finally, in 2003, the Navy pulled out of Vieques as well. Now all the Spanish Virgin Islands are on the path to recovery.

Sort of. For, as Teresa explains, one struggle has ended and another has begun. Not all Culebrans are good stewards of their island. Until nesting sites were made off-limits, the locals would collect birds' eggs for their own consumption, dramatically reducing the populations of such species as sooty terns. Ranchers would turn loose their cows and horses to graze on crucial habitat. They not only consumed rare flora but deposited in their dung the seeds of invasive species such as mesquite and acacia. And even worse, Culebrans have built countless squatter shacks in the mangrove-lined bays. This not only strips the habitat of crucial vegetation but introduces human waste into the fragile waters. Echoes of what happened to La Parguera.

That is why Teresa is so passionate about the work of the Youth Conservation Corps. Not only are they helping Culebra's wildlife refuges through their work, but also they are serving as models of good environmental stewardship to their families, friends, and neighbors.

Teresa indicates on a handout map the places I should see. When talking about Culebra, she speaks in exclamatory sentences.

"You *must* visit Puerto del Manglar! That's where the kids are planting the mangrove seedlings today. You'll want to go at night, though, too. That's when the waters glow. They're bioluminescent and absolutely *amazing!* And if you have time, try to visit Playa Resaca. It's a bit of hike. You have to go up and over Monte Resaca, but the waters are rough and wild and wonderful! You can just sit there and watch the waves breaking on the beach. And not far from here is Playa Carlos Rosario. Just offshore are these stunning coral reefs. You can snorkel to them right from the beach! And then there's Playa Flamenco. Flamenco was just named one of the best beaches in the world by the Travel Channel. That's a must-see!"

I haven't left the office, but I'm already exhausted from the proposed itinerary. I decide to visit Flamenco Beach first. Not because of the rave review, but because we share a history. It was just off Flamenco where Governor Ferré's private yacht was almost shelled by a gunnery crew. And it was here where the *Maroho* was chased off by a Navy patrol boat.

The road to Flamenco Beach leads past a large freshwater lagoon. Tricolored herons and white-cheeked ducks cavort in its waters. The pink flamingoes, though, have not been seen in years.

Flamenco Bay itself is shaped like a scallop. Its Aqua Velva blue waters lap gently against sands of blinding whiteness. It's a classic. There are a couple of sunbathers stretched out on the sands, and a family of picnickers at a table under Australian pines. A pair of skinny horses appear out of nowhere and trot along the water line. Other than these few visitors, I have the best beach in the world to myself.

I stroll the water's edge and come upon a rusted Army tank partly buried in the sands. It's now camouflaged with graffiti, including the crude rendering of a fish skeleton and abstract symbols in gold and green. The tank looks like a monument left by an ancient civilization. "Look on my works, ye mighty, and despair!" proclaimed Ozymandias.

Just above the beach sits another tank. It's entwined by a band of yellow tape, like the kind that marks a crime scene. The yellow tape extends from either side of the tank through tangles of sea grape bushes. Beyond this low-lying forest, the hills of the peninsula can be seen. It is a stark landscape of cacti, scrub brush, and giant milkweed. The land is still pocked with craters from the shelling. Here and there can be seen the rusted remnants of military hardware and stray balls of barbed wire. A sign warns in Spanish and English: Danger. No trespassing. Unexploded shells in area.

It's been more than thirty years since the last shell was fired on Culebra, and yet there are still areas where unexploded ordnance lies hidden in the sands or amongst the mangroves or on the coral reefs. It's a sad commentary on human nature that we seldom consider the long-term consequences of our actions, especially regarding the environment. How many years will it take before the PCBs are finally dredged up from the muddy bed of the Hudson River? How many decades before the forests are restored on the strip-mined hills of West Virginia? How many centuries before we've removed the billions (soon trillions) of tons of excess greenhouse gases from the atmosphere—if ever?

On a hill above Flamenco Bay stands the Navy watchtower, once known as Big Mary. A dirt road leads up to it, but the road has been closed since the 1970s and is now overgrown with thorny vegetation. A cloud of mosquitoes swirls around me as I hike up the hill.

The watchtower has long been abandoned. Graffiti artists have left their signs, symbols, and initials inside and out. From its large rectangular windows there are views in all directions. Through one window I see Flamenco Beach, the lagoon, and the hills of the peninsula. Through another I see Luis Peña, the island I witnessed being shelled by fighter planes so many years ago. I imagine what it must have been like to be the officer of the watch. One moment enjoying vistas of a tropical paradise. The next, their very destruction.

I step out on the observation deck. The railing's gone, and it's a rather steep drop below. But oh, what a view! I can see all the Spanish Virgins and beyond. Islands beyond islands.

But one alien feature stands out. It's the old military communications tower jutting up from the highest hill. The tower is so twisted and mangled and bent out of shape that it's hard to believe that it ever served some purpose. It's Eiffel gone mad.

I spend the next few days venturing all over the island, checking off the places on Teresa's must-see list. And while it's tempting to wax poetic about the colorful reefs, the luminescent waters, and the spectacular sunsets, the real beauty of Culebra lies in the more prosaic sights. A baby sea turtle paddling through a seagrass bed. Flying fish bursting from a moonlit bay. A frigate bird soaring over fan-leafed palms. A fisher tossing a bait net into crystal waters. And a young girl planting seedlings in a mangrove lagoon.

Before taking the ferry back to the mainland, I wander over to the town plaza. Lovers sit on benches and watch the sea lapping against the stone bulwark. Roosters and stray dogs scurry about. I see that the Alcaldía, the old city hall that overlooks the plaza, has been given a fresh coat of lime-green paint. Tough, twisted wind-blown trees guard its entrance. Somewhere a boom box is blasting Latin rap music and I think, *nineteenth century . . . meet the twenty-first.* The plaza is filled with young people. But I'm delighted to see also a weathered, old Culebran repairing a net. He sits in the shade of the ancient mahogany tree where many years ago his fellow citizens met to vote the Navy off their island. Perhaps the old man was there. I wonder how many young Culebrans today are aware of that wonderfully audacious act. And how it made possible the island they enjoy today.

In 2008, a memorial event was held in the plaza for Richard Copaken, Culebra's legal champion, who died too young of cancer. Kind words of praise and admiration were offered by his old friend Ramón Feliciano, now in his eighties. Feliciano served as mayor of Culebra for twenty-two years. And many of his dreams for the island have come true. There is a thriving ecotourism industry. Culebra's sheltered bays now harbor sailboats instead of warships. The island's stunning beaches are open to all. Its wildlife refuges attract naturalists from all over the world. The spectacular coral reefs are now a prime destination for scuba divers.

And for those who seek to commune with nature at its most elemental, there is a quiet cove where nature lovers can simply listen to the whispering of the sands.

"My dukedom since you have given me again," said Prospero, "I will requite you with as a good thing; at least bring forth a wonder . . ."

At the airport in San Juan, I see a vaguely familiar figure. It is Cruz-Cruz. I haven't seen him in years. His once-erect bearing is now stooped, but he still has that fire in his eyes. He doesn't recognize me until I remind him I was the captain he hired so many years ago. His brow furrows. "Ah, *sí! Capitán*," he says, and we shake hands. Then I ask about the *Maroho*.

"The *Maroho*. *Ay*, the *Maroho*." He shakes his head. "She is gone now. She is gone." The *Maroho* had been moored off Las Croabas on Puerto Rico's east coast when a tropical storm swept through. Her mooring lines snapped and the boat was never seen again. "I think she is resting," Cruz-Cruz says. "Resting on the bottom of the ocean."

But I have another vision of her fate. The *Maroho* was simply swept out to sea, where she was drawn into the Vieques Current and carried northward. She must have made it through the gauntlet of reefs and rocks off Cabo San Juan, since no wreckage of the boat has ever been found. From there, and for long days, the *Maroho* would have floated gently westward with the North Atlantic Drift. Somewhere off the Lower Bahamas, a spur of the Gulf Stream would have carried her north-northeast for hundreds of miles and into the blue-black waters of the Sargasso Sea. The boat is there now, I am sure—drifting, ever drifting, in the Limbo of the Lost.

Her faded pink superstructure is a rest stop, no doubt, for migratory seabirds making their annual journeys thousands of miles across the Atlantic. Sandpipers, plovers, and terns find the R/V *Maroho* an ideal place to rest, to feed, and to shit. Columbus crabs and sea spiders scurry about her rusted engine. Her orange hull, encrusted in barnacles and enmeshed in sargassum weed, is home to countless pipefish and anglerfish, sea anemones and dove snails, elvers and octopi. The *Maroho* is a floating sanctuary for marine life.

Which is about all the damn thing was good for anyway.

FIN

Selected Bibliography

Babín, María Teresa and Stan Steiner, eds. *Borinquen: An Anthology of Puerto Rican Literature.* New York: Vintage Books, 1974.

Cerame Vivas, Máximo. *Atlas Costero de Puerto Rico.* San Juan: Atlas Costero de Puerto Rico, 1988.

Cintrón, Carmelo Delgado. *Culebra y La Marina de Estados Unidos.* Rio Piedras: Editorial Edil, 1989.

Coll y Toste, Cayetano and José Ramírez-Rivera. *Seleccion de Leyendas Puertorriqueñas.* Mayaguez: Ediciones Libero, 1979.

Gallo, Cristino. *Language of the Puerto Rican Street.* Santurce: Book Service of Puerto Rico, 1980.

Hernández, Joseph Deliz. *How to Speak Puerto Rican.* San Juan: VB Publishing, 1998.

Lewis, Oscar. *La Vida: A Puerto Rican Family in the Culture of Poverty—San Juan and New York.* New York: Random House, 1965.

Paiewonsky, Michael. *Conquest of Eden 1493–1515.* Rome: MAPes MONDe Editore, 1991.

Picó, Fernando. *History of Puerto Rico: A Panorama of its People.* Princeton: Markus Wiener Publishers, 2006.

Robinson, Kathryn. *The Other Puerto Rico.* Santurce: Permanent Press, 1984.

Rouse, Irving. *The Tainos: Rise and Decline of the People Who Greeted Columbus.* New Haven: Yale University Press, 1992.

Steiner, Stan. *The Islands: The Worlds of the Puerto Ricans.* New York: Harper & Row, 1974.

Wagenheim, Kal and Olga Jimenez de Wagenheim. *The Puerto Ricans: A Documentary History.* New York: Praeger, 1973.

About the Author

Raised in New York's Hudson Valley, Kevin McCarey worked as a merchant marine deck officer and oceanographer. He quit life at sea to study filmmaking at the University of Oregon. Upon graduation, he worked on the Peabody Award winning series Portrait of America (TBS) and won Emmys for writing and directing. His documentary *Trumpet of Conscience* and narrative short *San Juan Story* were both Academy Award semi-finalists. Recently he's written and supervised films for National Geographic, such as *Sea Monsters*, *Tigers of the Snow*, *Dolphins: The Wild Side* and *Roar! One Man's Pride*. He now teaches filmmaking at the Savannah College of Art and Design.